COLLEGE

Real & Relatable Devotionals for Every College Girl

Jordan Lee

Formatted and edited by Katie Erickson

ISBN-13: 978-1541100107
ISBN-10: 1541100107

CONTENTS

Leader Guide:

An Exclusive Guide for Leading a Small Group or Bible Study in College

hey girl!

College can be so hard, can't it? The four years I spent at Indiana University were full of growth, challenges, exciting experiences, and more. I'm sure you're walking through a similar experience.

Throughout this series, I've chosen to keep it incredibly real. You'll learn about the times I fell flat on my face, made mistakes, and about the transformational experiences God allowed me to have as He drew me closer to His heart.

When I stepped onto the campus of a big, secular university my freshman year, I never would have guessed that I would come to know Jesus on such a personal level by the time I stepped off campus on graduation day.

I wrestled. I made mistakes. I wasn't perfect. But God took His time on me. He drew me closer and closer to His heart as the years went on. I hope to help you experience Him and His tangible love, even in a place that makes it incredibly difficult to do so.

Also, I want to add that I don't care where you stand now. If you've been faithfully walking with Jesus for years or if you're just curious about growing in your faith, you're welcome here. If you feel unworthy of being a Christian or would be embarrassed if your friends knew you were doing a devotional, we can keep it between us for now. This is a safe place – a place for you to come, be encouraged, wrestle, ask questions, and grow. Isn't that what college is all about anyway?

So, welcome. In this series, you'll find ten different topical studies. Instead of daily devotionals, these are weekly. I've designed it this way for two reasons:

1. I know you're busy. I know life is stressful and I don't want to add more to your plate or overwhelm you any more than you already are. I don't want you to feel as though you're falling behind on your devotionals because you have too much going on. God put it on my heart that one study per week would be manageable and practical for both groups and individuals going through this series.

2. These devotionals are written to accommodate group studies, although they work for individuals, too. They are designed to be a resource for those of you wishing to start a small group or Bible study in your organization, sports team, Greek house, or social group. The leader guide included in this bundle discusses in detail why these studies are shorter (3-6 weeks) in length. During my time leading a Bible study in my sorority, I learned that shorter topical studies make it more manageable and strategic when leading group studies with college students.

Thank you for diving into this adventure with me, with God, and with your friends (should you choose to lead a study). I pray that this proves to be a transformational resource for your walk with God in the middle of your college and early adult years.

Dear Girl in College Trying to Shine Jesus or Start a Bible Study in Her Sorority or Social Group and Struggling

I'm writing this leader guide *for you* because I've been in your shoes. I spent *months* Googling, praying, and searching for some resource created specifically for my situation.

Let me explain.

I went to Indiana University – a huge party school with one of the biggest Greek systems in the nation. Somehow, I ended up IN that Greek system, although I SWORE I'd never join a sorority. It's funny how God leads us where we don't want to go and then flips our lid with His purpose while we're in that place.

Maybe that's not your story. Maybe you've always dreamed of wearing letters across your chest. Or maybe you're not in a sorority but in some other social group, club, or team. Whatever your story may be, if you're reading this, I assume you're ready to learn how to make an impact, how to leave a legacy, and start a flame for Jesus in one of the most difficult places ever to do that – college!

I'm not going to sugar coat anything. I'm simply going to tell you what worked for me and what didn't work for me during my years in my sorority. I'm going to put tools in your hands that are equally simple and powerful at the same time. I'm going to force you out of your comfort zone. I'm going to strip you of the typical Sunday school Bible Study mentality, and equip you for a unique, yet incredibly rewarding, type of ministry.

Why? Because I believe college students are hungry for something more than Friday nights and 8 am classes. I'm convinced they still long for God even though they may not realize that's what they're seeking. They're searching for purpose in their studies and successes, for satisfaction in their relationships, and for acceptance in the party scene. I know because I've been there, lived it, and seen it transformed by the power of the gospel.

College ministry is strategic because if we can equip the next generation of leaders – the largest group with quicker access to the globe at the touch of a button on their smart phone than any other generation before them – then I believe that we can change the world with God's help.

So, we're going to meet people where they're at instead of expecting people to meet us where we're at. We're going to be real, raw, and relatable – and then invite our sister into that conversation.

NOTE: Throughout this guide and study series, you'll see me refer to my friends as sisters because I was in a sorority. However, that was just my individual experience. Feel free to exchange that with teammates, roommates, classmates, friends, etc., whatever fits your individual experience.

My Story

When I first joined a sorority, I had just begun to explore my relationship with Jesus. Although I was a baby Christian, I had all intentions of being a light for Jesus in a dark world.

I got my bid on a Tuesday and remember thinking, "YES! Now I have a platform! I'm going to share Jesus with everyone!"

I met a hundred girls on bid night and part of me was still hesitant about the whole 100-screaming-girls-living-under-one-roof idea, but I decided to give it a chance.

Then, Friday came. Friday was the first party. It was a luau-themed pair with a fraternity on campus. The night, my intentions of sharing Jesus seemed to flush down the drain with every drink I had. The excitement grabbed hold of me and I nearly passed out drunk the very first party I ever went to.

I woke up the next morning feeling like a complete failure.

How can I be a light to these girls now? They've seen me screw up. I'm no different from the rest of them.

You see, the problem is that I was turning my ministry into my own performance rather than God's perfection. I was more focused on taking credit for good behavior and showing others what it meant to behave, rather than showing them the grace of God.

But God had other plans. Over that semester, I learned a lot about the reality of His righteousness. I learned the importance of humility and grace, and how God would be sure I understood this had nothing to do with my perfection and everything to do with His purpose.

He taught me that even when are faithless, He is faithful (2 Timothy 2:13). What I thought would be a failure, the Lord used for good. He gave me strong fellowship to lift me out of the discouragement and shame and showed me how to love and relate to my sisters. As ugly as that drunken night was for me, even though I failed to start off on the right foot, I realized my pride was squished and I had to begin at a humble place.

Tim Keller says it well: "The gospel humbles us into the dirt yet exalts us into the heavens."[1]

I wasn't above anyone; I could identify with their struggles, their shame, and their mistakes. But I was called higher and deeper. Slowly the Lord drew me nearer to His heart, forcing me to rely on Him when peer pressure sunk in, rather than on my own morality.

Let me be clear, I'm not saying to go out and get hammered in order to be relatable. Not in the slightest. But I am saying that God has the power to use our past and perceived failures for His glory when we lay it at His feet. So, if you feel like you've blown it, lay it at His feet because He can and will use you. It's not about how qualified we are. It's about how willing we are.

Over the time that I lived in the sorority house, He challenged me to focus on loving. God taught me early on that my own righteousness is incredibly insufficient. He challenged me to rely on His righteousness instead.

Sometimes people would roll their eyes, and I had to learn to love them and realized Jesus loved them too - even when it felt like I was being persecuted. I shouldn't have been surprised, though.

Keep in mind that while you're leading, you are going to face opposition. Jesus said, "If the world hates you, keep in mind that it hated me first." (John 15:18).

Over time, I learned that I just had to own it. I had to own that I was one of the Christian girls in the house and that some people just wouldn't understand that.

I also had to make sure I wasn't untouchable. In other words, I had to be vulnerable. I had to be open and honest about the mistakes I'd made in the past, the way the Lord redeemed them, and even share the things I struggled with in the present.

I also learned that I had to be available – I lived in the sorority house my senior year and I'm so glad I did. Those months in the house allowed me to connect with younger girls in younger pledge classes that I otherwise would not have known. We met over coffee, snuggled up and talked on the couch for hours, and we simply became friends. Part of leading is putting others before ourselves, and sometimes that means sharing with them what they desperately need to hear or staying up until 2 am helping a sister after she's had too much to drink.

The craziest thing is that there wasn't anything overly structured about my ministry. I was simply investing into girls because girls had invested into me.

I still praise God for those two seniors who started the Bible study the year I joined my sorority, and they passed it onto me. I still thank Him for the girls who took it over after I left and continue to pass it on.

I've been told that the Bible study has continued to flourish in a house that had just started Bible study the year I joined. NUTS. My drunken self in a Hawaiian shirt at that luau party would never have guessed how much God would turn a failure into a victory. I believe God wants to do that in your house or group, too. I believe God wants to use you and that He's challenging you to take steps of faith that you may feel unworthy of.

I challenge you to let GOD transform your heart, to grow you in big ways, and to love your friends enough to hear their story and share His story with them.

Be Approachable

There's a lot temptation in college. When I really started walking with Jesus, I wanted to avoid it at all costs. I got comfortable in my Christian circle and I didn't really want to hear about hook ups and what so-and-so did last night. It began to make me cringe and broke my heart. For a little while, I felt like I was one of the only ones who understood God had so much MORE for us than that. So much BETTER!

I began to notice myself getting judgmental. I started to believe the lie that I was *better than* instead of *better off*.

There's a difference.

As Christians, we believe we are better off than non-believers because we have the sweetest gift – SALVATION! Being better off is different than being better THAN. For example, just because a rich person is better off than a poor person, in terms of finances, the rich person's value and the poor person's value are no different to the Lord. Both are humans with dignity and rights and it'd be a capital offense if either one were killed because we know that ALL life is valuable.

If you know Jesus and if you're living a Godly life, remember that although you are spiritually richer than those who do not know Jesus, you are not better than your friends who may not know Him.

When the Lord showed me this profound truth, I was humbled. He showed me in His Word how Jesus never compromised His mission, but He never failed to meet people where they were. He was approachable, relatable, and humble. He reclined with the drunks and tax collectors

(Matthew 9:10), He talked to people who were considered "less than," and ultimately, He loved. He loved big.

If we're following the model of Jesus' ministry, we can't walk around with a prideful crown on our head as if we are a princess who is better than everyone else. The closest thing to a crown He ever wore during His ministry on earth was a crown of thorns.

So, what's that mean for us? It means it'll be hard. It'll be gritty and not too glamorous. We'll spend our time at lunch listening to our sisters' stories. We'll go where they go. We'll go places that the world says Jesus would never go. We'll go to frat parties, we'll hold our sister's hair when she pukes, we'll go to bars, we'll listen to her drunken struggle, we'll share our own struggles and stories, and we won't judge.

Why? Because there's a negative stigma about Christians on college campuses. I've heard over and over that college students don't want to be "religious" because religious people are stiff, boring, and judgmental. But if we are truly holy, we need to realize that "holy" does not mean uptight, religious, or figured out.

It means perfected by the only One who is perfect. That's not something we can accomplish by means of behavior or religion – only by way of surrender and humility.

If we're more relatable than we are religious, if we're more Christ-like than we are critical, then we will be approachable. We've gotta be friendly but not fake. We've gotta be real but not religious.

Some simple ways to be approachable are:

1. Gather where they gather.

2. Join the conversation.
3. Be vulnerable; show your flaws and be open.
4. Let them see you "out." Honor God and don't be a hypocrite or drink yourself silly, but show them you're not too good to go where they go.
5. If you don't feel like you have the self-control to go out, take time to be ministered to and grow in your faith. We all need help, too.

Be Available

One of the times I saw God move most was second semester of my senior year. I lived in the sorority house and I'm pretty certain I was one of the oldest girls still in the house. Typically, seniors live out of the sorority house and there were many days I wished I wasn't sleeping in a bunk bed anymore. But when I graduated, I was so grateful for those months.

I had a lighter workload than previous semesters, so I was able to hang around the house a lot more. I was able to get to know girls in the younger pledge classes and eventually invited several to coffee. We chatted for hours as they told me their story, their struggles, and more. Other girls began knocking on my door or texting me for advice with the guy they were dating or other frustrations they were facing. I decided early on not to limit what I would talk about. If they wanted to talk about drinking, we'd talk about it. If they wanted to talk about sex, we'd talk about it. If we needed to cry, we would cry.

To be honest, there were many times I wanted to close my door and not listen to the drama – and sometimes I did (you *do* have to know your limits). But I know that even when I had to force myself to listen, listening mattered. Listening is one of the simplest ways to love because it requires time and attention – something people really get very little of in today's world, especially in college.

As a Christian on a college campus, I realized that investing in people with time and love was even better than influencing them with good behavior they could observe from afar, because investing DID influence them on an incredibly personal level. It's exactly how Jesus went about ministry – He invested in the men who opened their door to Him.

When you're considering how to do ministry in your sorority or on your campus, don't over-complicate it. Ministry can be very simple. Build time into your schedule for others – for that girl you've wanted to invite to coffee or the one you've been feeling could use a simple girl's night over movies and popcorn.

Consider the women God has laid on your heart. How can you make yourself available to them? Start by encouraging them with a simple text or invite them to lunch. Making yourself available as a friend will build trust and fellowship as well as open up avenues for strong conversation and opportunities to share the gospel.

Have an open door policy. As you build relationships, make sure you emphasize that you're always available to chat. Invite girls to come hang out in your room, dorm, or apartment – just because. Make yourself available and I promise that you will have more conversations as you invest in their lives.

As you build trust, those conversations and opportunities will arise because girls will feel comfortable opening up to you. When they do, speak into the pain or struggles they have shared with you with the hope message of the gospel. A simple way to be prophetic, or to witness, is to share a piece of your story that relates to hers, how you saw God move through that, and offer the hope that He can do the same for her. This is a very natural and honest way to begin spiritual conversations and share the gospel.

Starting a Bible Study

I spent a whole week preparing for the first Bible study that I led in my sorority.

I hung a sign on the door and announced Bible study at our chapter meeting. Although some girls rolled their eyes, I got through the announcement without dying of embarrassment. *Phew!*

The first meeting rolled around and I was READY! I even had a nifty little navy blue folder packed with notes and all sorts of devotional guides and questions. I tabbed the passages we would be reading from and had my favorite context clues highlighted. I didn't want to leave anything out.

Since I was so prepared, I was confused when I walked away from the first meeting feeling completely discouraged. The conversation was stiff and awkward and I felt more like a teacher talking to my pupils than I did a peer talking with her friends. I could see by the looks on their faces that they weren't interested in returning anytime soon. I hated it. I wanted to quit. I felt like I was from Christian outer space and I wanted to hop on my rocket ship and fly home.

I took a step back and asked myself some hard questions:

Why was the conversation so stiff?
What did I do wrong?
What do these girls really want – and need?

These are the questions I want to answer for you: the things I wish I had known when I was in college, and the tips that really make a small group meeting abundantly FULL.

What Did I Do Wrong?

When you're starting a Bible study in an environment that may be some level of hostile toward the gospel, you have to be strategic. College campuses, even Christian colleges, are one of the more diverse places you can set foot into. Combine that with the overarching stigma across campuses that Christianity is boring and uptight and you're up for a challenge.

The first place I went wrong was assuming I had to take on a teacher role. I made the study about how much Biblical knowledge I had and could teach instead of making the study about who Jesus is and what He could do through our lives.

I didn't have a defined strategy or goal. I was prepared, yes. But I was prepared for something structured instead of something transformative.

I also dove right into a semester long study on the book of Ruth. Great idea in theory, but I realized that I had to be more realistic. College women have so many commitments as it is. To ask them to commit to something else, especially something that indicates more studying, is a recipe for disaster. It's even more intimidating when it's a long-term commitment. Instead, I should have started small, introducing shorter studies with shorter commitment times. For example, when I chose to introduce a four-week study, I noticed many more girls were willing to jump on board because they didn't feel the obligation to commit their whole semester, and girls felt as though they could join halfway through because it was easier to catch up.

Ironically, what started as a short-term commitment turned into a long-term commitment. Once they experienced one short-term study, many were hungry for more and came back for the next short-term study.

This is not about pressing your Biblical knowledge onto them. It's about sharing Jesus in a simple, tangible, and loving way. Keep it simple and honest. Start small.

When starting a Bible study, you should keep two goals at the forefront of your mind:

1. Encourage those who are already walking with Jesus.
2. Attract and encourage those who don't know Him or who have lost touch with Him.

It's amazing what a good conversation, informed by the gospel, can do to accomplish both of these goals.

Why Was the Conversation So Stiff?

The conversation was stiff for a number reasons.

1. The environment was stiff. We were gathered around a table as if it were a formal classroom.
2. The conversation was more like a quiz. I would ask a contextual question from one of my nifty little guides and wait for someone to raise their hand with the proper response, which many hesitated to do out of fear of being wrong.
3. I didn't make room for messy. I didn't let the conversation flow or encourage the girls to share how the message we had just read personally impacted or related to them. I didn't allow them to wrestle, ask hard questions, or open up. I stayed on task, making sure to get to every question, instead of letting the questions get to us – to the heart of the matter.

I decided to change my approach. I chose to host Bible study in my room and I made my announcements more inviting. Instead of saying, "Hello, ladies. Join us for Bible study where we will be studying the book of Ruth all semester," I began to say, "Hey guys! I know it's a long semester and we're all overwhelmed and stressed out. Feel free to come hang out with us on (insert day) at (insert time) to unplug, talk, and encourage each other in our faith. It'll be really chill. Anyone is welcome – wear your pajamas, bring hot cocoa, and join us!"

I shouldn't have been so surprised when my room was packed full the very next Bible study meeting.

I also changed the structure of the conversation. I stopped worrying about if we got to all the questions and instead let real conversation happen. I gave the girls time to think and encouraged them to share personal parts of their story in relation to what we had just studied. I opened up and shared pieces of my story. We prayed for each other. We began to create a dialogue that wasn't centered around being right but about being real.

When hosting or leading a small group or bible study, be sure to make meaningful conversation with your friends a priority. This has to be real conversation, the kind of conversation that lifts your soul, builds strong relationships, and that is open, honest, encouraging, and informed by the gospel.

What Do These Girls Really Want – and Need?

I thought the girls needed to learn new Bible verses, memorize them, and regurgitate them. I thought they needed more school.

But they don't want more school. They don't need more school. They need more of the Spirit. They need the simplicity of the gospel that speaks truth and life over their weary souls.

Think about it. Consider how tiring and stressful college is when you know Jesus. Imagine how much more difficult that must be without having the hope of an eternal resting place and peace the Savior brings.

Create a safe place for these women. Some of them may be long-time believers, but many of them may simply be seeking. You've got to start simple. You need to start small. You need to show your brokenness and be okay with not knowing all the answers.

You may be leading the small group, but you are still their friend. They want and need friendship. They need to see that they aren't alone, they need to hear your story, they need hope, and they need the gospel.

By being a friend, introduce them to the friendship and acceptance Jesus invites us to step into with Him.

Shift your focus from talking at them to talking with them. Listen to their story. Identify what may be holding them back from trusting God. Encourage and love them through that. Watch how the avenues for sharing more and more of Jesus with your group will open up in ways you can't even imagine.

The Meeting Structure I Found Most Successful

1. If the girls know each other, start with casual conversation, have each girl share a high and low of the week. If not everyone knows each other, start with introductions and then have each girl share a high and low of the week.
2. Dive into the devotion/reading.
3. Ask the corresponding questions, allow some time for thinking, and be okay with silence. If no one answers, be vulnerable and share a story.
4. Turn to the Word and review what truth says.
5. Allow for more conversation. Ask if they have any thoughts or questions after reading the verses.
6. Pray it out. Hug your friends. This is supposed to be fun!

Bottom line: Let it flow! The most successful studies I facilitated had an unstructured structure. The most important things are opening the Word and having meaningful conversation.

Now What?

You have resources! I've written ten short, topical studies that are designed to accomplish all that I just shared with you when it comes to leading a small group or Bible Study on your college campus. There is one study per week to accommodate one group meeting each week.

Each study has a handful of questions that are made to cultivate conversation. When asking them, keep in mind a couple of things:

1. Give them time to think and to muster up the courage to answer.
2. Don't be afraid to share your answers, too – this is a conversation, not a quiz.
3. It's okay not to get to every question if time doesn't allow for it. Conversation can continue as you move on to studying the verses in the study section.

The Bible verses presented in each study have been prayerfully chosen to speak right into the issue or challenge presented. The verses are referenced and explained but they are not quoted word for word in the study so that the group has the opportunity to actually open their Bible and go see what that verse says before learning about it.

Make sure you have the group dig into the Word, open their Bibles, and find each verse before skimming through the explanations of them. Use the explanations as a tool but do not rely on them. The Word itself is the most powerful and informative resource you can give these girls – and for many of them, this may be the most exposure they've ever had to the Word.

Create conversation. Keep it comfortable, real, and simple. But above all else, crack open God's Word together.

Party on Purpose:

A Powerful Perspective on Parties, Peer Pressure, and Purpose

Hey girlfriend!

Welcome to the party!

I'm so excited because this study is going to give you a super real life look into partying. I'm taking you to real parties with me, because I've made mistakes in my life, too.

I know the party culture is rough in college. When I tried it on for size early on in my college years, I felt icky and unfulfilled when I'd have a bad night (like the ones you're about the learn about). When I got to know Jesus, the desire to party seemed to dwindle, but when I chose not to go out, I often felt left out and lonely. I worried that people thought I was uptight or a boring Christian girl.

Maybe you're the party girl right now, afraid of what your friends would think if they knew you were going to a Bible study. Or maybe the party life isn't fulfilling anymore and you're looking for something more. Or, you've walked away from the party life and aren't sure what to do next. Perhaps you're feeling isolated or bored.

So regardless of where you are in your faith journey or your opinion of partying, your brokenness is welcome here; your worries and shame and questions are welcome here.
We're going to work through it together and discover the realities and truths tucked beneath the surface of the party culture that college smacks us with the day we set foot on campus.

We're going to be real about the hard stuff, honest about the yucky stuff, and turn to Truth in the middle of it all. I'm going to tell you real stories of mine and I expect you not to judge but to see the redemption in the midst of it. I expect you to be honest with your own journey through the social life that college offers (whether you party now, used to party, or have never even been invited to a party).

We all come from different places, have different testimonies, and share different experiences that affect our decisions. But I hope that at the end of this, we will find some common ground in Christ Jesus and be encouraged in one simple truth: regardless of our past or our present, God invites us to a bigger, better party in eternity. Together, we're going to discover how to RSVP.

Xox,

jordan lee

For more, follow me online!
Facebook: **Jordan Lee**
Instagram: **@soulscripts**
www.thesoulscripts.com

week 1: welcome to the party

Psalm 37:4
Galatians 1:10
Revelation 19:7-9
Romans 5:8

I found myself on a sticky fraternity floor and held my breath
as the cheap beer made its way into my mouth and down my
throat. I heard chants and cheers all around me. I felt a
strange combination of guilt and pride all at once.

I was being cool – a rare thing for me. I shook off the guilt,
chugged down the cheap beer, and basked in the attention.
Someone snapped a picture that I still look back on from time
to time. It somehow serves as a messy memory that reminds
me of where I once sought approval from: drunk people in a
basement with neon lights and sticky floors.

Lovely.

Maybe that's your story, maybe it's not.

Maybe you're thinking, *what's the big deal? I do that every
weekend!*

Or maybe you're like, *OMG... HOW DOES SHE HAVE A
MINISTRY NOW?!*

Regardless of where you are in your faith journey, what your
status in the party culture is, or what your reaction to the
situation I just shared is, I'd be willing to bet that if you did a
little reflecting, you'd find some way or another that you've

been overwhelmed with pressure to do what the world wants you to do, even if it damages your tiny, beating heart in the process.

Any maybe, just maybe, you've caved.

If you have, you're not doomed. You're a broken human. You're a broken human seeking affirmation and approval just like every other human on this planet. And if you're anything like me during my first year of college, you may be willing to hurt yourself just to get it.

It was a short period of my life, just a few months, but those few months taught me a whole lot about how much we crave approval.

Isn't it crazy how important it is to be affirmed, accepted, and applauded? It's like our DNA was wired to need love and approval more than anything else in the world.

Popularity often masks itself as love. But real love doesn't ask you to be popular. Instead, it *gives* you purpose.

Anyway, here's my point: I know sometimes that the pressure to fit in can really get to us. Sometimes the desire for acceptance gets twisted and we end up in really sticky situations (see what I did there?).

But you know what else? It's a far better thing to stand up and stand out than to fit in.

If you're stuck in that sticky basement, not sure how to get up or afraid of being judged, remember that you already have approval. You don't have to compromise your character to impress a crowd.

Why?

Because you're invited to a better party – to the greatest party there is, hosted by God Himself under a big sparkly banner that reads, CHOSEN, REDEEMED, LOVED, ADORED, and ACCEPTED DAUGHTER OF THE KING.

Won't you join me there?

TALK IT OUT

How have you felt pressure to fit in or be someone you're not? What have you changed about yourself to do so?

Where or what have you been seeking approval from?

TRUTH SAYS...

Psalm 37:4 is an encouragement to seek the satisfaction we crave from God. When we delight in Him and when we walk with Him, He will satisfy our heart's deepest needs. The more we know Him, the more our good desire to be accepted will mirror the desire He has for us that we would know that the greatest acceptance our hearts need is God's.

Galatians 1:10 urges us to live in God's approval over living for people's approval, because that's the soul-sanctifying, eternal approval our hearts really need. When we accept Jesus, we're given His righteousness and God's approval.

Revelation 19:7-9 mentions the supper of the lamb. It's a party, a celebration for God's people united to Him. When we let Jesus be our Savior, we unite ourselves to God in a relationship like marriage. We are invited to celebrate that.

Romans 5:8 is a beautiful reminder of our acceptance. We were accepted without deserving or earning acceptance. While we were still on that sticky basement floor, Jesus gave up his life for us. That is love, and it beats every cheer and chant from frat boys.

THE BIG IDEA:

YOU AM INVITED TO A BETTER PARTY AND
THE HOST ACCEPTS YOU AS YOU ARE

week 2: hold my hair

Galatians 5:22-23
Proverbs 4:23

Last week you learned about a time I drank a lot of cheap beer on the sticky floor of a fraternity basement in an effort to be fun and cool. A few weeks later, I attended another party.

In an effort to maintain my "fun" reputation, I consumed far more alcohol than my small body could handle. Same story, different day. Only this time, the results were much worse.

I quickly lost my sense of control and my friend had to call a cab. On the way home, my body rejected the alcohol. Without my consent, the champagne and liquor came back up as fast as they went down. Embarrassing, I know.

Sorry, taxi driver.

I bet you didn't think you'd be seeing this in a Bible study, did you? But this has a purpose and it's about being real here, so stick with me.

Eventually, I made my way home, struggled into clean clothes, and crawled into bed. I felt nauseous through the entire night. I walked back and forth to the bathroom as my body continued to reject the junk I put in it.

The smell of sweat and vomit mixed together, creating an aroma that only added to my nausea. At this point, I began to think that maybe the chants and cheers weren't worth the five minutes of fame.

Maybe you've been in this situation. Maybe you've never touched a drink in your life. But that's beside the point.

The point is that when we put icky stuff in our bodies, even ickier stuff comes back out. Similarly, when we put ugly stuff in our hearts, ugly flows out from it.

When we fill our mind and lives with things that discourage and destroy us, we're going to be discouraged and maybe even feel destroyed.

But we're not stuck there. We're not left hopelessly hanging over a toilet. Do you know why? Because when we confess our brokenness, Jesus lifts us up, cleans us off, and loves us through our crazy, stinky mess.

TALK IT OUT

Consider your recent surroundings this semester.

What has been filling your mind, heart, and body? In what ways have those things either encouraged and uplifted you or discouraged and defeated you?

Has joy, peace, patience, and goodness flowed from your heart? Or have anger, doubt, and discouragement flowed out from your spirit?

This is a safe place. Don't be afraid to lay it all out there.

TRUTH SAYS...

Galatians 5:22-23 describes the fruit of the Spirit. Fruit is good stuff produced as a result of a soul planted in the rich soil of the Spirit. When our soul soil is full of pesticides, short on water and Son-light (get it?), it will be difficult to produce these good things. Filling ourselves with Truth in the midst of a discouraging environment can bring about peace, patience, love, etc.

Proverbs 4:23 reminds us to guard our heart because everything we do flows from it. Think about it. In this story, what did I do? I put a LOT of toxins in my body. As a result, what came out? More toxins. And while I'm not condemning the occasional glass of wine, it's important to guard our hearts from all things that are toxic to our joy. This isn't just about too much alcohol, but it also applies to things like comparison, overworking, gossip, and more.

THE BIG IDEA: PUT GOOD IN, GET GOOD OUT

week 3: replenish

John 6:50-71
1 Corinthians 10:4
1 Peter 2:2

If you've been going through this study, then you know that at this point of the story, I'm drowning in my misery after a night of one (or five) too many drinks my freshman year of college.

If you're just hopping into the study, here's what you missed: Peer pressure got to my freshman heart, I drank too much, and ended up sick all night as a result.

--

The next morning, I woke up with a wicked hangover. I felt like I had just been hit by a bus, run over by a train, and wrung out like a sponge. My body felt empty and lifeless and my head throbbed. I explained how exhausted my muscles felt to my roommate.

She, being a pre-med student, explained that I was probably dehydrated and suggested that I needed to get some nutrients in my system. I wasn't sure if I felt like eating or crying or both, but I figured she was probably right.

I poured myself a tall glass of orange juice and grabbed a bottle of water, two slices of bread, and three Advil. I curled up in the fetal position to let the nutrients fix my dehydration.

Within an hour, I began to regain my strength. I was able to eat a nutritious lunch, nap again, and by the evening, I was even able to go for a walk outside.

If we look at that recovery process, it's obvious how important physical nutrition is when we are dehydrated.

I believe that we can experience spiritual dehydration without even realizing it – especially in college, where half the campus is dehydrated every weekend.

When the enemy gets the best of us, when He whispers lies into our head and urges us to do something that actually harms our walk with God and our spiritual strength, it's as if there's a spiritual hangover that can make us feel weak.

We may begin to feel drained or weak in our faith or relationships. We might even have a headache or a heartache just trying to recover from life's messy nights (and those don't necessarily involve drinking).

This story is used as an example, but anything can dehydrate us spiritually. It can be family issues, tragedy, hardship, loss, heartbreak, stress, and so much more.

So, if you're feeling spiritually dehydrated, if you're not feeling strong in your faith or close to God, don't forget the importance of nutrition.

Spiritual nutrition comes from mustering up the courage to get up out of bed, pour a tall glass of OJ, sit down and talk to Him. Read His Word. Let Him work.

Throw some Jesus jams on. Replenish with good things when you're feeling dehydrated.

Sooner rather than later, you'll regain the strength to keep walking in sync with your Maker.

TALK IT OUT

In what ways have you felt exhausted or dehydrated in life?

What has been dehydrating you spiritually? In other words, what is causing these feelings? Is it peer pressure, an unhealthy relationship, inadequacy or low self-esteem, or stress? Identify what's giving your heart a hangover.

TRUTH SAYS...

John 6:50-71 are the words of Jesus describing Himself as the bread of life. Just like the pieces of bread I ate helped revive my body, Jesus revives our spirits and gives us eternal life, something bread made with flour simply cannot do.

1 Corinthians 10:4 explains that spiritual drink, or hydration, flows from the Rock. Jesus is the Rock, and when we take time to connect with Him, He heals our dehydration.

1 Peter 2:2 speaks of spiritual milk that a baby would need to growing up strong. The imagery here describes the journey of the faith walk with God's Word as our nutrition for growing stronger. He is the ultimate resource when we are dehydrated, weak, and unable to keep walking (just like when I woke up with a wicked hangover). As we let His Word and His ways into our hearts, especially when we feel as though all hope is lost for us, we will mature and grow stronger so that we can walk with Him.

CHALLENGE:

For groups: pray over the girl to your right. Specifically, lift up the burdens that she has shared that are dehydrating her heart and ask God to replenish her spirit.

For individuals: write down the specific areas of your life that are dry and need replenishment. Pray for peace and life when you feel like you are a walking hangover.

THE BIG IDEA: REHYDRATE YOUR HEART

week 4: fresh start

Lamentations 3:22-23
2 Corinthians 5:17
1 John 1:9
Ephesians 1:7

At this point, I had consumed far too much alcohol too many times in an effort to feel cool and comfortable in a crowd of strangers. Eventually, my body rejected the alcohol and I threw up everywhere. Then, I woke up with a wicked hangover and felt miserable until I replenished my body with nutrients.

But then IT happened. My friend told me her version the night, the blurry parts my mind didn't recollect from the night before when I woke up the next morning.

I said WHAT to WHO?! Please tell me I didn't actually take a cigarette out of that guy's mouth and violently throw it on the ground. Please tell me I didn't give that guy my number. I tried to run away? You're joking. Oh, you're serious? Wow. Oh my gosh. You've gotta be kidding me.

I apologized and laughed it off, because I wasn't sure what else to do. College told me it was no big deal. It's funny, right? Not really.

I honestly wanted nothing more than to crawl under a rock and pay rent to the rock troll until the end of the semester. I couldn't believe I had to be taken care of! I couldn't believe I said such hurtful things to people I barely know. The cops could have caught me for publicly drinking under age. I couldn't believe that I was stupid enough to rip a cigarette out of a man's mouth! I could have gotten punched!

WHAT IS WRONG WITH YOU, J?

I asked myself this for days. I got stuck in a mindset that told me I screwed up and there was no fixing it. I felt embarrassed and disgusted by my inability to hold it together. I wanted a do-over.

I wanted to go back, un-live, and relive that day. Time machines hadn't been invented yet so I honestly thought I was out of luck. I sulked around for weeks, avoiding any type of social life because I was afraid of making a fool of myself again.

A few weeks later, I just happened to be at the same building where a campus ministry was meeting and I just happened to overhear the speaker dude talk about shame, and I just happened to step inside the door.

I don't remember much about it, but I do remember two profound things that He said:

1. "Guilt says you've done something wrong. Shame says you are something wrong." (Sheila Walsh)[1]

WOW! That hit me hard. I realized that I wasn't just experiencing guilt but also carrying shame around and letting it be my entire identity!

2. "God's mercies are new every morning." (Lamentations 3:22-23)

Wait. Is this the fresh start I'd been searching for?

You betcha. That day was a turning point for me – a fresh start. I began walking with Jesus and getting to know God. The more I did, the more He gave me strength to keep walking although I had (and still have) a lot of learning to do.

Do you want to hear the best news? I'm no different from you. You don't need a time machine. A fresh start is available for you, too, sister.

Every. Day.

TALK IT OUT

Have you ever felt the feelings I've described in this week's story?

How have you handled those feelings?

What makes it hard for you to believe that all things are redeemable?

TRUTH SAYS...

Lamentations 3:22-23 says that we are not stuck when we make mistakes going to make mistakes if we surrender them to God with a humble heart. This isn't just a free pass to do whatever we want knowing He will forgive us, but it is a message of hope that when our brokenness begins to rule our hearts, it doesn't have to define our lives. You can celebrate, you can party on purpose, with purpose, because His mercies are new EVERY morning!

2 Corinthians 5:17 says that He sees you where you are. He sees your struggles, your hangover, your heartbreak, and your shame. He looks at it and says, "if anyone is in Christ, (s)he is a new creation." Know what that means? You're not stuck, and your mistakes or behaviors don't define you. When you place your identity in Jesus, you are made NEW. New mercies, new identity... *this is good news*!

Ephesians 1:7 tells us that we have redemption through His blood.

1 John 1:9 tells us that we get that redemption the moment we confess our sins and get up from our place on the floor to keep walking with Him. There are no qualifications other

than surrender. When we let Jesus be Lord of our life, it influences every decision we make.

If you like to party, maybe you've just been celebrating the wrong thing. Maybe you've been celebrating junk instead of Jesus. And if you don't like to party, maybe you've forgotten to celebrate all who Jesus is and what He's done for you. You see, God doesn't tell us not to party, He just asks us to party in a different way – in a way that's full of life, free of shame, celebrating His love for us. We don't need a sticky frat house floor or cheap booze to do that. You're invited to a better party, an eternal party that never ends.

Celebrate *that* party with purpose, on purpose.

THE BIG IDEA:
HIS MERCIES ARE NEW EVERY DAY –
CELEBRATE THAT!

We've come to the end of the study on partying. Maybe it was what you expected, or maybe not. Regardless of how it met your expectations, I hope you walk away from this study encouraged. I pray that this study has helped you to realize four big things:

1. Your identity is not in people's approval.
2. God invites you to join His party.
3. He will replenish you when life wears you down.
4. God redeems all things, and your mistakes don't define you.

No matter what your level of activity in the party scene has been, remember that there is one party that you're always invited to.

Now it's up to you to decide if you want to accept the invitation. He's waiting to greet you with open arms.

Chill Out:

Mastering School, Stress, Future, and Success with Faith

Hey girlfriend!

If you're here, I'm assuming that you're burdened, burned out, or bummed out by the pressure to perform.

College is hard. It's a weird time in our lives where we experience the largest combination of education and exploration at one time. It's a place with a heightened expectation of us to try things, to be well rounded, to succeed, and to prepare for the future.

When I was a student at Indiana University, I distinctly remember feeling like I had to have my personal and professional life figured out or I'd fall behind. In the beginning, I was afraid to choose a major that I wouldn't like because I thought that if I chose the wrong thing, I would hate my work after college and be miserable. Later on, I questioned how qualified I was for prestigious internships and jobs in comparison to my peers. I worked my butt off in an effort to give me an edge in a field I wasn't even sure was for me.

Why? Because college said I had better figure it out.

I know, these four years are hard. And it doesn't necessarily get easier when you get out of school. But I hope the next six weeks help you step back, breathe, and see the bigger picture. I hope you are encouraged to let go of what you can't control, trust God in the process, and examine your purpose in the midst of papers, parties, and professional programs.

You can breathe. Your life won't crash and burn if you don't like your major, or if you don't know what you're doing after you graduate, or if you don't have a power packed your resume.

So over the next six weeks, let's stop working so hard at worrying – and put our energy in better places.

Whaddaya say?

Xox,

jordan lee

For more, follow me online!
Facebook: **Jordan Lee**
Instagram: **@soulscripts**
www.thesoulscripts.com

week 1: Lost

Psalm 119:105
John 16:13
Matthew 6:24-25

Ever feel like you're in an episode of Lost? I have.

When my parents dropped me off at my dorm my freshman year of college, I felt like I had just been dropped in the middle of a jungle. I had to figure out how to survive in a whole new environment, packed full of all sorts of dangers.

I wasn't sure what direction to go when it came to picking a major, choosing clubs, making friends, or all the other things that were essential to college survival.

I made my way through the journey over the years, I experienced various challenges, and I encountered beasts of all sizes – tough exams, mean professors, peer pressure, and more.

As I approached the end of the journey, just before I reached the finish line, I freaked out.

What's next for me?! What am I going to do next?

I didn't have a solid plan. I had invested so much time and energy in survive the jungle, I hadn't thought about what I would *do* once I got out of the jungle.

Maybe you're feeling that now. Maybe you're afraid to take a wrong turn – whether that's choosing a major or taking an internship. Or perhaps you see the edge of the tree line in the distance and you're starting to feel the stress that a new transition can bring.

If you feel like you're walking in the dark and scary jungle, stop freaking out. Reach down deep in your backpack and find your flashlight and your compass. Your flashlight will illuminate the step in front of you, and your compass knows which way is north and which way is south. If you follow it and keep walking forward in the Light, you will reach your destination.

Because His word *will* be your flashlight – a lamp unto your feet and a light unto your path – and His Spirit will be your guide. The reality is that if you know Jesus, you'll arrive at the one destination that really matters when this life is said and done. So, enjoy the journey – He's already got it all mapped out.

TALK IT OUT

What causes you to feel the most fear or anxiety about the future?

Do you worry about choosing the wrong "thing"? The wrong major, the wrong friends, the wrong internship, the wrong social group, or the wrong job?

Have you invited God into that worry? If so, how? If not, how would you like to?

Groups: pray for each other's worries!
Individuals: write down your prayers over each worry!

TRUTH SAYS...

Psalm 119:105 reminds us that although we may not see the whole journey ahead, God is always faithful to illuminate the step before us.

John 16:13 tells us that when we feel lost and unsure of where to turn, the Spirit will be our guide.

Matthew 6:24-26 is Jesus' reminder to stop worrying about the future, to be present now and focus on today, because God will take care of tomorrow and meet our every need.

THE BIG IDEA: YOU ARE NOT AS LOST AS YOU FEEL

week 2: discover your purpose

John 13:34
1 Corinthians 10:31
2 Timothy 1:9

I ordered my sub and she got to work. I asked for extra pickles and she rolled her eyes. I requested light mayo and she sighed heavily.

It was obvious that she wasn't happy. It could have been a number of things that made the woman on the other side of the counter so irritable. As I shuffled through my wallet looking for my credit card, I wondered what it could be that made her so irritable.

Did I say something wrong? No. That can't be it. I just asked for pickles.
Maybe she has a headache or a bad rash.
Maybe her boyfriend broke up with her.
Hmm... what could it be?

I looked up to hand her my card and I got a glimpse into her eyes. They were empty, worn, and weary. Somehow in that moment, I knew exactly what was buried deep inside. God made her heart's cry so clear to my heart.

There were so many things I wanted to say to encourage her, but in the moment I couldn't seem to find the words. A line had started to form and she turned to help the next customer before I could gather the proper words.

I took my sandwich, tucked my card away, and walked out to

my car. It killed me that I couldn't speak into her pain. But I'd be willing to bet you might be feeling what she felt that day, so here's what I would say:

I'm not mad at you for your poor customer service. I know you're tired. I know you feel purposeless from where you stand. I know you question the value of your work, and I know you're sick of the grind. I know that you wonder if you matter or if anyone sees you. And I know that as you ask the same questions to each customer, pacing back and forth behind the counter, that you question your purpose and worth every day. I feel you, girl.

*I know that you think you didn't make a difference in my life. But you did. You did because you gave me fuel to keep working today. You gave me fuel to keep living my tiny purpose of encouraging other girls to keep living their purpose. It's a beautiful chain reaction that I don't want you to overlook. So, to the lady feeling useless, purposeless, and weary: Your purpose is simple but mighty and **never** insignificant because it keeps others going. I just think you ought to know that.*

TALK IT OUT

Have you ever felt like the sandwich shop lady? In other words, do you ever feel tired of the routine this life demands of you, or like you don't know what your purpose is, or how you can possibly make a difference?

What small opportunities to live out a simple purpose of investing in others for God's glory have you overlooked in your daily life?

For groups: turn to the girl to your left and point out two gifts, talents, or strengths you first notice about her that she could be using to fulfill her simple purpose every day.

For individuals: write down a list of your gifts, talents, and strengths that you could be using to fulfill your simple purpose every day.

TRUTH SAYS...

John 13:34 says that if you are loving others in whatever way your gifts allow from right where you are, you are living your most important purpose. It's difficult but it's simple.

1 Corinthians 10:31 reminds us to live for God's glory and fixate on His bigger purpose in the simplest of things. Even if we are making a sandwich behind a counter, we are serving His people. When we shift our perspective from our own glory to God's glory, we will no longer be concerned with WHAT we are doing but instead with HOW we are doing it.

2 Timothy 1:9 says that we are called to a holy calling. Too often we forget that holiness is associated with humility. The mightiest purpose is planted in the humblest of hearts. Don't be surprised if you don't get much attention for your work. That's not what it's about.

THE BIG IDEA: DON'T OVERLOOK YOUR SIMPLE PURPOSE

week 3: when life gets stormy

Psalm 46:1-3
Psalm 91:2
Mark 4:39-40

It was a sunny Sunday afternoon in college. I threw on my tennis shoes and went for a jog. I ran down the street and rejoiced in the beautiful sunshine. But to my dismay, I saw dark, grey clouds rolling in when I turned the corner. They seemed far enough away for me to finish my run and make it home before the storm hit.

I'm sure you can guess what happened next.

I was wrong. *So wrong.*

Within fifteen minutes, I was miles away from my house and surrounded by angry storm clouds. I picked up the pace in hopes of making it back before getting drenched.

I didn't make it. Not even close. Before I had a chance to take shelter, the clouds took a big dump on me. The street began flooding. Lightning began flashing and the thunder rolled. I wiped the rain out of my eyes and scanned my surroundings. The closest covered area was a parking garage a half-mile away.

I ran towards it as fast as I could. When I finally got there, I took cover, just in time, too. The winds picked up and the lightning was getting closer. I watched the storm roll through from the safety of the cement shelter.

It seemed to pass as quickly as it came. The clouds broke, the rain ceased, and I was able to finish my jog home.

When I think about that day, I realize how accurately that memory reflected the reality of my life in college. I remember feeling like as soon as the sun would shine, an unexpected storm would hit, and before I knew it I would be drowning in work, pressure, deadlines, and stress. There were so many times I felt as though I couldn't escape the rain before it hit.

But there was a parking garage – a strong, safe shelter. I saw it and I ran toward it with every ounce of energy left in my weary legs. I was safe from the storm there, wasn't I?

I don't know what kind of storms you are facing. Maybe you're drowning in schoolwork or struck down by one of life's tragic lightning bolts. Maybe you feel disappointed, discouraged, or maybe even depressed.

Wipe the rain out of your eyes and run to *The* Shelter. You can take refuge in Him when the stress levels flood the streets of your mind and when the storms of life try to knock you down.

TALK IT OUT

What storm are you currently running through or have you recently run through?

Where did you take refuge, or in other words, to what or to whom did you look for help? Was it God, or something else?

Do you have trouble trusting that Jesus can not only comfort and keep you, but also calm the storms of life? Why or why not?

TRUTH SAYS...

Psalm 46:1-3 tells us that God is our refuge and help in times of trouble. When we are overwhelmed, overworked, or troubled, He is the safest place for us to take refuge.

Psalm 91:2 says that God is a trustworthy fortress. The big, cement parking garage may have been strong enough to weather the storm, but God is stronger than the storm itself.

Mark 4:39-40 reminds us that Jesus has the power to calm the storms in and around our hearts if we let Him. He has power over all things; our job is to believe that He can and will.

THE BIG IDEA: GOD IS OUR REFUGE

week 4: make room for rest

Psalm 46:10
Matthew 28:11-12
Mark 2:27
Hebrews 12:1

I'd be willing to bet $10 that you're probably stressed and you're probably overwhelmed and you're also probably a little cranky.

Great, now that that's out on the table, let's see what we can do about it.

College is hard because it challenges us to explore – to try new things, to do a lot, and to discover what we like. It's awesome and awful at the same time.

It's awesome because who doesn't like to try new things? And what better time than when you're young without too many responsibilities?

But it's also awful because in trying new things, it can be very tempting to try to do *everything*.

Between the obligatory school work, a social life, leadership programs, memberships, clubs, intramurals, and internship or job searching, it leaves little time for our souls to rest and very little room in our hearts for Jesus to hang out. Our heart is His home address that we need to make hospitable. All too often, we clutter up His house when we fill it with all sorts of other junk.

Bob Goff says, "every Thursday I quit something."[1]

I want you to imagine quitting something. I know it's not the popular thing to talk about in an environment that says, *"winners never quit & quitters never win."*[2]

While that's true to some degree, this isn't about quitting at everything or quitting at living a purposeful life. It means quitting things that don't matter—shutting off distractions. I think we need to examine what we're trying to win. Are we seeking to win an earthly race or an eternal race? How can we really win if we don't take time to rest our legs? We're going to burn out. It's a marathon, not a sprint.

Although I don't suggest giving up or throwing in the towel, don't forget that it's okay to cut out the extras that are weighing you down. Quit little things. Quit the late night social media scroll. Quit seeing that guy that's taking your time but not touching your heart. Quit saying yes to everything.

God created us to need deep soul rest. The very thing our souls need most we deprive them of far too often. But if rest is the most important thing then we ought to give ourselves permission to cut something out to make room for it.

TALK IT OUT

Do you tend to bite off more than you can chew?

When was the last time you experienced true peace deep in your soul?

What small things can you cut out of each day to make room for more of Jesus?

TRUTH SAYS...

Psalm 46:10 tells us to be still. Be sure to read this verse in context by reading the entire psalm. It is not merely a suggestion but a command. God takes rest seriously and we need to as well. The command to "be still" literally in the Hebrew language (which it was originally written in) means to stop what you're doing. The "know that I am God" command is the most intimate form of knowing a person. It refers to being in intimate relationship with God, So, this verse tells us to stop all the distracting stuff you're doing and be in intimate relationship with God.

Hebrews 12:1 urges us to run the race with endurance and to press on toward Jesus. Being a Christian in this world is a hard race to run as it is. It's going to wear us out. But it's more important, more rewarding, and worth more than any other race we could sign up for. Stop at the water stations on the sidelines to rehydrate with the living water. Fix your focus on the finish line, and the little hills along the way won't seem so long.

Matthew 28:11-12 is a powerful invitation from Jesus to approach Him regularly and He will lighten our burden. The rest we need is found in Him alone.

Mark 2:27 highlights something important. The Sabbath, the day of rest, was made because God knew we needed it. He did not make us for rest but He made rest for us.

THE BIG IDEA: DO YOUR BEST AND LET YOURSELF REST!

week 5: the president of everything

Psalm 85:8
1 Peter 5:7
Philippians 4:7

One year in college, I was home for Christmas break and something crazy happened. While eating dinner, we heard a big pop coming from the basement. Upon running downstairs, we discovered water dripping from the ceiling. My dad sighed in frustration and said that a pipe must have burst.

I asked how that happened and he explained that the water pressure must have gotten too high, or something like that. I really didn't understand the technicalities of it, I just remember that there was too much pressure on the pipe because of the cold and it caused it to burst... I think. That's what I'm rolling with for now, anyway.

I also remember thinking how much I had felt like that pipe the previous semester. I had been under so much pressure not only to succeed at my academics but also to succeed at everything. I was on the leadership team for campus ministry, I worked part time, I led a committee on a scholarship program, and I somehow juggled a social life and campus ministry leadership position.

Just days before the pipe burst in the basement, I had burst into tears and curled up in the fetal position in bed after finishing finals.

"It's like college expects you to be the president of everything," I told my mom. "I'm expected to balance leadership and studying and management and prepare for my professional future and somehow do fabulous at all of it. It's so much pressure!"

She comforted me until my tears ceased and my breathing calmed.

I spent the remainder of Christmas break mending my busted heart, and my dad spent the remainder of Christmas break on the phone with the plumber (sorry, Dad!).

The plumber came to our house, fixed the busted pipe, and adjusted the pressure so that it wouldn't burst again. I realized how much Jesus acts as the plumber in our lives, mending our hearts and fixing the pressure levels with His peace when we call Him.

So, if you're feeling the pressure to be the best at everything, if you're juggling far too much and about to burst (or if you've already burst), please realize that you have a trustworthy Plumber to call on. He will mend your heart with a peace that transcends all understanding.

TALK IT OUT

What has put pressure on you recently?

Have you burst, or are you on the verge of bursting?

How much have you invited the Master Plumber into that situation? Have you allowed Him to fix your broken pipes with His peace, or have you been trying to operate with big holes in your heart?

TRUTH SAYS...

Psalm 85:8 says that God promises peace to His people, to those who turn to Him, serve Him, and trust Him with their lives.

1 Peter 5:7 tells us to cast our anxieties and all the pressure we are under on Jesus, because He cares deeply about our hearts.

Philippians 4:7 is God's promise that His peace is so powerfully able to guard our hearts from bursting again that it transcends beyond our understanding. I didn't understand how the plumber fixed the pipe in our basement nor do I understand the intricacies of God's peace at work. All I know is I trusted that the plumber who fixed the pipe knew what He was doing, and I can trust God to fix my heart in the same way.

CHALLENGE:

For groups: Pray for peace over the girl to your right.

For individuals: Write down your prayer for peace in your journal and then speak it out loud. Declaring truth over our hearts by visualizing and vocalizing our prayers helps to internalize it.

THE BIG IDEA: GOD IS THE PLUMBER WHO MENDS THE PIPES IN OUR HEARTS WHEN THE PREASURE BREAKS THEM

week 6: purpose over practical

Jeremiah 29:11
Proverbs 16:3
Matthew 6:31-33
John 2:1-11

A friend recently asked me the following question:

*I'm really struggling. I'm trying to decide if I should pursue my passion or pick a more practical career that will allow me to provide for myself. **What should I do?***

Here's my response:

*I can't tell you what to do. But I can tell you what I **did**. When I chose a major and a career path, I took the safe route – the route that makes sense to the world. I picked a practical career path that basically guaranteed me a secure job after college. I was on track to begin a solid job in the world of Healthcare Administration upon graduation. I had it all mapped out. I felt secure yet unfulfilled. But guess what happened? I still ended up living my passion. Regardless of how much I tried to plan and control my own future, God still paved the way and led me straight into His purposes and plans for my life – practically. I am able to provide for myself despite not staying on the "practical" career path.*

God will have His way one way or another if you have an open and obedient heart, and He will provide. Know why? Because the dreams you have didn't pop up out of nowhere. They are so intentionally unique to you because the Author of your life story planted them deep within the walls of your heart. So instead of worrying about being practical, trust the

God who is powerful. Trusting God and following His will sometimes looks backwards to the world, but that's often where His power really shows itself. So, shake the dust off and discover what God has etched on your soul. Then, peel those etchings off and stick them on your mirror until they become so undeniably a part of who you are that you can no longer run from them.

Stop being afraid of getting it wrong. Stop being afraid of what the world might say or the million ways you could fail. Fail away. God will use each little failure for a mighty triumph. Know why? Because the very best way to win in this life is to follow the path He's designed for you, even when it's unusual, uncertain, and unconventional. Turn those etchings into action and take a risk.

Because your dreams are no coincidence.

Stop living in fear and start acting in faith. Watch what God will do.

TALK IT OUT

What do you think God is calling you to do? In what ways are you taking steps to put that into action?

Do you have a dream or passion that the world says is silly to pursue because it seems financially unreliable?

What holds you back from taking steps of faith toward your passion or toward discovering your passion? Your parents' or friends' opinions, a busy schedule, discouragement, or something else? Share it with the group (group study) or write it down in your notebook (individual study).

TRUTH SAYS...

Jeremiah 29:11 is a verse that we hear often but it holds a powerful truth that beckons us to open our hands, move our feet, and live in faith. God has already mapped out our life. He has great plans to prosper us when we are obedient. Prospering doesn't necessarily mean in terms of finances or the worldly idea of prosperity, but God will instead prosper us in ways that further His Kingdom, and He will do so in His timing. When we feel the tug on our hearts to make a change, we can rest assured that He has a plan for that change.

Proverbs 16:3 encourages us to commit our work to the Lord, because when we do, our plans will be established. He will guide us into His very calling when we invite Him into our work and open our hearts and minds to His will.

Matthew 6:31-33 tells us to seek first the kingdom and then *"all these things"* will be added unto you. *All these things* are the needs we worry about having met – if I pursue something that isn't practical, will we have enough to eat or drink? When we worry about if we will have enough money, God knows our every need and He is faithful to provide. We can take risks and step inside His plans with confidence that He will give us all the things we need when we put our gifts to work for His kingdom.

John 2:1-11 is the story of Jesus' first miracle, where He turned water into wine at a wedding. If you look at verse 7, you'll notice something profound: obedience is measurable. The servants filled the jars *to the brim* with water. As a result, they got jars filled *to the brim* with wine when Jesus miraculously turned the water to wine. They had plenty for the remainder of the wedding feast. This shows that we get back what we give to God. If we give God everything, if we give Him our best and trust His hand over our life, He will give us His very best.

THE BIG IDEA: GOD'S WILL MAY NOT LOOK PRACTICAL, BUT IT IS ALWAYS POWERFUL

Perfector > Perfection:

3 Weeks on Beauty, Brains, and Body

Hey girlfriend!

I'm so pumped that you're here!

This is a shorter, but equally as important, study with the rest in this series. From my experience at a big university and in a sorority with hundreds of beautiful women, I know comparison runs wild in college. I remember feeling like I never quite had the right hair or outfit. I lived as a slave to the scale. I'd eat too much pizza and worry about how my jeans would fit. It took me years to find a good, healthy balance between developing a healthy and fit lifestyle and not becoming a slave to it.

This study is designed to touch on struggles all women face with body image and confidence. If you have a rockin' bod, that's great. But I know it tends to feel like it's never enough even when everyone else says it is. I know because I lived it. The gym became my jail even after I lost all the weight I hoped to lose. If you feel a little soft and squishy, it can be far too easy to slip into body shaming. I know because I did that, too, so much so that I starved my body because I began to hate every imperfection more than I cared about my health.

For years, I felt as if I couldn't avoid comparison. I never quite felt pretty enough when I would look around at other girls on campus, in my sorority house, and at social events.

Maybe you haven't recognized your struggle in this area yet. Maybe your self-confidence is through the roof. Maybe you feel like you always have to put yourself together. And maybe you feel gross because you often don't take the time to put yourself together. It really doesn't matter because at the end of the day, the reality is that we all compare and we all want to feel beautiful.

So, we're going to talk about it over the next three weeks. We're going to look in the mirror and embrace what God gave us. We're going to look into the eyes of our sisters and see the beauty they hold within. We're going into the Word to see what God sees in us and what He has to say about it.

If you're fat or skinny or tall or short or blonde or brunette or red head or blue eyed or green eyed or brown eyed or some beautifully unique combination of all of those, you're welcome here. Because I get that the outside is important – but it's not the beauty that impacts the world.

I hope the next three weekly studies fill your heart with joy while God's Word fills your heart with the true, real, life-changing love and truth that we all need.

Xox,

jordan lee

For more, follow me online!
Facebook: **Jordan Lee**
Instagram: **@soulscripts**
www.thesoulscripts.com

week 1: not-so-bikini-body

Proverbs 31:30
1 Corinthians 6:19-20
1 Timothy 4:8

The week before spring break of my freshman year, my friend and I went shopping for new swimsuits. I stood in the dressing room, tried on a pink bikini, and looked in the mirror.

Woah.

The "Freshman 15" was showing itself for the first time.

I picked my body apart:

My thighs have gotten so jiggly!

Oh my gosh. My arms are huge.

Is that cellulite on my butt?!

I have to do something!

To be honest, it really wasn't that bad. But insecurity took my heart captive and ate it for lunch.

I went home that night and researched diet plans, weight loss tips, and get-skinny-fast schemes. I found a blog that told me that in order to lose weight, you have to burn more calories than you consume. I got to work right away. I downloaded a calorie-tracking app and hopped on the treadmill.

Somehow, I managed to run two whole miles. I could hardly walk the next day but hey, I was off to a great start!

At first I simply planned to get healthier by exercising daily and eating less sugar but it quickly became an obsession.

I eventually lowered my daily calorie intake so low that I would have been considered clinically malnourished. I continued to run long distance and exercise excessively without upping my calorie intake. I even stopped going out to dinner with friends because I was afraid the menu wouldn't offer a meal under 250 calories.

It only got worse when my grandma passed away and my relationship with my boyfriend began to crumble. I wanted to feel attractive, but I also needed control when other things in my life started to spin out of control.

Ironically, the more I controlled my calorie count, the more my calorie count controlled me.

I denied I had a problem because it wasn't the typical eating disorder you hear about on TV. I was still eating and I was not making myself vomit. I was simply driving myself into malnourishment in secret. Nothing wrong with that, right?

Later on, I learned that I had a "Restraint" eating disorder. It took months and months to find freedom when I finally recognized and accepted that I did indeed have a problem.

By the grace of God, my health was restored, as was my relationship with Him.

Looking back, I see the reality. In the midst of starving my body, I was also starving my spirit because I became completely consumed with my exterior. I was starving for beauty and control. What I did not realize was that I already had God-given beauty and a good, good Father who is in total control, even when the circumstances around me spun out of control.

From someone who has lived through the shackles that the lie that perfection places on our heart, let me remind you: it is important to stay healthy, but your body is not your identity. It's the temple of your true identity.

Keep it a healthy home for the Spirit to dwell, but please do not starve it in order to look a certain way. Just as a homebuilder designs a home how he sees fit, God designed you how He sees fit. If you let Him, He will come and make His home in your heart. Then, it will not be your body that gives you your sense of beauty or worth. It will be His Spirit.

TALK IT OUT

Have you ever felt self-conscious of your body type or weight? Have you compared your body to other women's?

If you've wrestled with an eating disorder or unhealthy relationship with food, share it with the group or write down your story in a journal. Even if you have not wrestled in this way, share or write down what causes your spirit to feel empty or starved like mine was.

Have you made your heart a hospitable home and your body a healthy temple for God's spirit? Or have you obsessed over it for your own glory?

TRUTH SAYS...

Proverbs 31:30 says, "Charm is deceptive, and beauty is fleeting; but a woman who fears the Lord is to be praised." In other words, when we make the Lord our first priority, our focus becomes less about looking beautiful for people and more about becoming beautiful because of God living in us.

1 Corinthians 6:19-20 holds a profound truth, that our bodies are temples of the Holy Spirit. Our bodies are Holy Spirit's dwelling place and something to be honored, taken care of, kept healthy, and treasured – not damaged by obsession with perfection.

1 Timothy 4:8 reminds us that training for the kingdom is more important than physical training. In other words, training your soul and strengthening your faith will prove to be more beneficial than obsessing over the number on the

scale in the long run. Don't lose sight of this when working on your physical health.

THE BIG IDEA: HEALTHY HEART > PERFECT BODY

week 2: Freshen up

2 Corinthians 4:16
1 Peter 3:3-4

I went back and forth to the hair salon FOUR TIMES in one week during college. Ridiculous, right?

Let me explain.

I had just moved into my sorority house. Upon seeing all the other girls, I immediately didn't like what I looked like. It seemed like everyone else had the prettiest makeup, the cutest hair, and trendiest outfits.

And then there was me.

Have you ever looked at everyone around you and said that? *And then there was me.*

Insert heavy sigh

My wardrobe consisted of Target brand shirts, old jeans, and gym shorts. My hair was pretty plain and I was sick of being so boring-looking.

In that one week, I spent over $350 of my hard-earned summer money just trying to switch up my look.

First, I went to the mall and bought some new dresses for class. Then, I went to the salon for the first time and dyed my hair blonde.

Too blonde.

So, I went back to add lowlights.

Lowlights added.

It looked better but as soon as I showered, it faded to a weird reddish color so I had to go back AGAIN just to fix it. In order to fix it, we needed to add a toner and dye it darker.

Toner added. Dark dye applied. Adios to my hopes of being blonde.

At this point I was frustrated. I didn't go through all that just to be back to square one. So, I went back AGAIN. Unfortunately, my hair was over processed and dying it wasn't an option at that point. You know what we did? We chopped it. We cut it and the stylist gave me a sassy little bob.

Finally! I feel fresh!

I left the salon with an empty wallet and a new air of confidence about me. Girls in the house commented on how cute my new cut was. I ate up the attention. But after a few days, the newness faded and I realized I didn't know how to style short hair.

The cycle continued. I even considered extensions until I learned how expensive they were.

Eventually, it had to stop. I was out of money and began to question what "me" even looked like.

Maybe you've been there. Maybe you've looked around at a crowd of beautiful women and felt totally inadequate. Perhaps you've done crazy things and spent crazy amounts of money just to freshen up your look like I did. It's a girl thing. I get it. We want to feel beautiful, and that's fine.

But here is my question: What if we spent as much time, energy, and attention as we do comparing and preparing our appearance as we spent preparing our heart? What if we poured our time, energy, and resources preparing for Jesus? Into knowing Him and letting Him shape our heart?

If I could send a letter back in time to my 20-year-old self, I would have challenged her to pause, to stop looking outside of herself, and to start looking inside. Because maybe, just maybe, her heart needed a new do more than her hair needed a new do.

But since I can't do that, I'm going to give that letter to you. Here's what it would say:

I know you want to feel beautiful, and I'm not stopping you from freshening up your look from time to time. Have at it. Buy the shoes. Get the lipstick. But don't obsess over it. Consider how temporary a fresh haircut or new lipstick is. It's only going to be fresh and new for so long.

*Take two seconds to stop comparing your beauty to the beauty of the world, because your beauty transcends **all** earthly things.[1] Your beauty is beyond flawless skin and style.*

So, if you are going to invest in something, invest in your faith more than you invest in changing your face. Invest in your relationships more than your reputation. Invest in your walk with God more than your walk. Invest in your inner beauty as often as you invest in your outer beauty. When you shape your eyebrows, consider how you're letting God shape your heart. When you trim your hair, consider what you could allow the Lord to trim around the edges of your heart.

I promise, your life, your faith, and your wallet will be richer for it.

TALK IT OUT

Has there ever been a time in your life that you felt completely obsessed with freshening up your exterior appearance? Did it fulfill your heart completely, or only temporarily?

CHALLENGE:

For individuals, write down the things about your appearance that you often wish you could change.

For groups, share with the group the things about your appearance that you often wish to change. Then, after each member has shared, speak encouragement into whatever that "thing" is for the girl to your left. Tell her what YOU see as beautiful that she isn't seeing. Do this until each person has been encouraged in her "thing."

For example, if the girl to my left's thing is that she often wishes she could change is her height, I would encourage her by saying I can relate but that I actually think her long legs are a sign of endurance. God built her for running the race of faith with endurance, and even if she's not a physical runner, He displayed that gift in her physical attributes.

TRUTH SAYS...

2 Corinthians 4:16 is a profound truth that speaks right into these feelings. When we feel plain, boring, or weary on the outside, He is renewing us on the inside. Godly, eternal renewal is the change our hearts are truly craving when we change our looks in hope of feeling fresh and new.

1 Peter 3:3-4 reminds us of the importance of God-given inner beauty and its lasting importance over external beauty.

THE BIG IDEA: I MAY NOT FEEL FRESH OR BEAUTIFUL, BUT I KNOW GOD HAS MADE ME A NEW CREATION

week 3: masterpiece

Psalm 139:14
Ephesians 2:10
Galatians 3:26-27

Imagine a beautiful painting with vibrant color and flawless brush strokes covering the canvas. There's not a drop of color out of place or a smudge to be seen. It may even be displayed in the Louvre, the world's most famous art gallery, renowned for some of the finest pieces of art in the world, including the Venus de Milo and the Mona Lisa.

Now imagine a painting done by a little girl in preschool. Smudges, clashing colors, and uneven strokes cover the canvas. It may not be the next Picasso and certainly wouldn't be something displayed in the Louvre. A fancy interior designer would likely advise against displaying the preschooler's painting. However, a proud parent would gladly hang it on the fridge for each and every guest to see.

Now think about that. One painting may have been deemed more valuable because of its presentation, but the two pieces were both works of art. They were both worth displaying and highly valued by those who love them.

You and I both know that the child's artistic ability isn't what earned her painting a spot on the fridge. Her painting got a spot on the fridge because his parents love *her,* not her work. Her father didn't say, "I love how perfect your presentation is. I believe that this worthy to earn a spot on my fridge."

That wouldn't make sense. Instead he says, "This presentation may not be perfect and it might actually hurt my eyes to look at. But I love you so I will *give* you a spot on the fridge."

When we know Jesus, God is no longer just God but Father. He is our parent and loves us *even more* than a parent would a child. He doesn't love our work or presentation. He simply loves *us* because we are *His* work – His handiwork. We only have a spot in His house through His work. Our place has been given, not earned, because of Christ's work on the cross.

When we are moved and melted by the gift of His grace, when we choose Jesus as our Savior and Lord, we are given a spot on the fridge. We don't earn it by our flawless reputation or presentation. It is given as a byproduct of the Father's love.

Maybe you know that. But don't you still get discouraged when you feel like a bad Christian? Don't you feel like giving up? I've been there, too.

Let's go back to the three-year-old for a moment. When a child creates a piece of art and her dad hangs it on the fridge, she doesn't fight them and say, "It's not good enough! I need to make it perfect first!"

On the contrary, she rejoices! He doesn't care how perfect or good it really is. So long as her dad says it is good, then it is good. What if we trusted God's opinion of our presentation that way? What if we weren't so caught up in perfection and instead captivated by the Perfecter – the one who sees His perfect Son when He looks at us?

When we become like children and let Jesus be our perfection, we will see that our appearance, presentation, or accomplishments are **not** what wow Him. *We* are what wow Him. We wow Him because we are the work of His hands.

Our messes don't define our worth, because our story is so much sweeter than the flaws we have in this life. He wrote our story, He created it Himself, and when He looks at us, He says, "I made her. I made her legs long and her hair curly. I made her curvy and freckled and passionate. I love every piece of my work. I will *give* her a spot in my house."

So, before we worry about whether or not we are primped, poised, and perfect enough, perhaps we should consider the fact that it's wasted energy to worry about those things. Because when we make Jesus our Savior and chase relentlessly after HIM, we still get a place on God's fridge, even when we're a hot mess.

Don't be a slave to the scale. You are not Princess of the Land of Perfection. You are a Princess, an heir of the King of Perfection. Be a servant to your Savior. That's the kind of *life* (not just body) that makes a *masterpiece*.

TALK IT OUT

Do you find yourself spending lots of time trying to perfect your physical presentation or academic and professional presentation? How does this leave you feeling?

What about your personality makes you feel unworthy, inadequate, or self-conscious? For years, I felt like I wasn't fun or outgoing or witty enough. What about you?

TRUTH SAYS...

Psalm 139:14 reminds us that we have been fearfully and wonderfully made. We are made by God's design and there's nothing flawed about that

Ephesians 2:10 says that we are God's handiwork and He has prepared for us good, meaningful, purposed works to do. If we took our eyes off the mirror and fixed them on the cross, we would discover a real life of fulfillment. The word for "handiwork" in the Greek here is *poiema*, which is similar to our English word poem. This word gives the idea that God composed and wrote us and chose each little piece, just like a poet chooses each word to sound just right.

Galatians 3:26-27 is the truth that when we accept Jesus, we are clothed with Him. When God looks at us, He sees Jesus. Our imperfections are made perfect in the eyes of God by His perfect love.

THE BIG IDEA: MY LIFE, NOT MY BODY, IS A MASTERPIECE BECAUSE IT HAS BEEN DESIGNED BY GOD AND SAVED BY JESUS

It's Complicated:

Dating, Dudes, & Drama

Hey girlfriend!

I'm so stoked you've chosen to do this study!

The dating scene isn't easy in college. Whether you're casually dating someone, head over heels crushing on someone, heartbroken, or somewhere in between, I pray this study opens your eyes to the bigger picture when it comes to relationships and your heart.

I think faith can feel like the challenges that come with dating. It can be hard to navigate and difficult to understand, at least without the right guide.

Maybe you don't know where you stand in the dating scene. Maybe you don't know where you stand with God. Maybe you're tired of hooking up with guys and looking for something more. Maybe you've never even kissed a guy.

It really doesn't matter, because wherever you are in your relationships on earth or with God, you are welcome here. If you're lonely or tired or weary or broken or thriving right now, you're welcome here.

This study is designed to touch on common issues and realities that come with dating, to guide you along in the best relationship there is: God Himself!

I pray my silly little excerpts and stories fill your heart with joy, while God's Word fills your heart with the true, real, life-changing love and Truth that we all desperately need.

Thank you for allowing me to pour my soul out in hopes of encouraging you, and for letting God lead you through this study.

You totally rock.

xox,

jordan lee

For more, follow me online!
Facebook: **Jordan Lee**
Instagram: **@soulscripts**
www.thesoulscripts.com

week 1: is there anyone for me?

John 15:16
Ephesians 1:4
1 Corinthians 6:20

Have you ever gone to an ice cream shop and had trouble picking the perfect flavor? You know, those times that you sample nearly everything in the freezer and the poor little ice cream shop employee starts rolling their eyes?

But that ice cream shop employee just doesn't understand.

I mean, we've spent time and energy just to get to the ice cream shop and now we're about to invest even more of our resources so we can really enjoy an ice cream cone. It's kind of a big deal.

Isn't it the most frustrating thing when, after all that taste testing, you can't seem to find a flavor that really suits you?

Cake or waffle? Bowl maybe? Toppings? Oh my gosh. This is so hard.

Now, imagine how hard it would be if you were the ice cream.

You'd constantly be in a state of, "Pick me! Pick me! I'm sweet and I promise it'll be worth it!"

When the ice cream shopper passes you up, your little ice cream heart might melt a little. *Ouch!*

Step out of the ice cream shop with me for a minute. I know this is a dramatic example, but I think it captures the way our hearts feel when we've been let down or when we've had a hard time finding a match. When we notice all our friends getting chosen, asked on dates, and crushed on, we begin to ask questions like:

What's wrong with me?

Or

*Is there **anyone** out there for me?*

After a while, it's easy to feel lost in the crowd and possibly even feel unwanted.

Maybe the guy you like picked a different ice cream flavor. Maybe you've lost hope in your own lovability. Or perhaps you've felt time ticking and rushed into choosing an ice cream flavor, or a relationship. Maybe you feel like you're settling.

Whatever your particular situation is, there's more.

There's more because the truth is that there *is* someone out there for you. Although it's normal and good to long for a guy to want you, he's eventually going to let you down and he won't satisfy your heart like you think he will now. He might even let you melt or drop you on the sidewalk.

But when God walks into the ice cream shop, He doesn't overlook us in the midst of all the other flavors. He doesn't wonder if I'm good enough; He makes me good enough. He picks me, without hesitation, and He picks you, too.

If you're feeling a little lost or hopeless or disappointed with dating, or if you're feeling a little unworthy of being purchased, hear this: that's exactly when He picks you. He scoops your heart up and takes you home. He's purchased you at a price, at the cost of His Son's life. He never overlooks you, never lets you melt, and never drops you on the sidewalk. Ever.

TALK IT OUT

In what ways have you felt overwhelmed by the dating scene?

Tell your story: what has caused these feelings? A broken heart? Losing friends to their boyfriends? Having a hard time getting a date? Share your story or write it down.

Be honest with this one: have you let God into the ice cream shop of your heart? Have you invited Him to scoop out those yucky feelings and scoop you up as His own? Or have you hung up the CLOSED sign on the door?

TRUTH SAYS...

John 15:16 contains the words of Jesus. Here He is speaking to His apostles, reminding them that He chose them. He brought them out of their old life and into a new eternal life with Him. He says the same thing to us – He chooses us. We are so dependent on Him, but sometimes we fail to see our need for a relationship with God when the world tells us we need romance with a guy.

Ephesians 1:4
Again, we see the recurring theme: God chooses us. He chose you long before the world began. He knew who you would be and what you would do, and He gave you the opportunity to be holy and blameless in love before Him by letting HIS love be your Savior from all darkness, instead of relying on a man to be your functional savior.

1 Corinthians 6:20 tells us that we were bought at a price. This is referring to the price Jesus paid on the cross to rescue us from death and restore us to God. He paid the price we deserved to pay and died in our place. When we make Jesus our Lord and Savior, the transaction is complete for us, too. Our life has been chosen and redeemed at a high price so that we can have a relationship with God.

THE BIG IDEA: THERE IS SOMEONE OUT THERE FOR ME. GOD CHOOSES ME WHEN I FEEL UN-CHOOSE-ABLE.

There's a God-sized hole in your heart. What are you trying to fill it with?

week 2: fighting for the heart

Deuteronomy 5:9
Deuteronomy 20:4

My freshman year of college, I went to a costume party dressed as the Cookie Monster. I wore an outrageous outfit complete with fuzzy blue slippers.

I was accompanied to the party by a group of friends I hung around with at the time, including the guy who I had recently started talking to. We weren't dating yet, though. We just went on dates and did all sorts of things dating people do but we weren't *together*. That would be far too serious.

During the party, I began talking with some girls in the living room and he walked into the kitchen where some of the guys gathered. Noticing his absence, I walked toward the kitchen to see what he was doing. When I turned the corner, I nearly flipped my lid.

What the heck does she think she's doing?

A girl dressed in stilettos, a mini skirt, and fishnet tights was dancing with him, and I don't mean square dancing. I mean dirty dancing. *Really dirty.* We weren't dating but jealousy oozed out of me as I glanced down at my hideous cookie monster outfit.

Dang it! Why didn't I wear something cuter than this?

"Oh boy," I said to my friend, "look at her."

Stiletto-mini-skirt-girl happened to overhear me.

"Excuse me," she shouted over the music, charging at me in her stilettos like a wobbly freight train. "What? Is he your *boyfriend* or something?!"

Unsure of what else to say, I shouted, "YES!"

I saw him smile out of the corner of my eye. He had heard me, and so did the rest of the party, so evidently, we were officially dating now.

Shoot.

"Well, I am so sorry to burst your bubble." she said sarcastically, "but you better watch your mouth next time!"

Her aggression sent me into a fit of nervous giggles.

She didn't like that, either, "you aren't going to be laughing when I give you two black eyes!"

Get it together, J. I'm good. **Everything is fine.**

I walked away with my blood boiling. Just when I thought it was over, I looked over my shoulder. She was following me!

Are you serious?

Someone tried to stop her, but she shoved him aside as she shouted another profanity. She told me how ugly I was, how I need to keep myself in line or she would have to teach me a lesson.

I don't know about you, but I don't handle threats very well. I was almost certain steam was literally blowing out the top of my head. You know, like in the cartoons.

The DJ cut the music, conversations had ceased, and a circle began to form around us. I heard chants, "Fight! Fight! Fight!"

Before I knew it, I found myself in the middle of the crowd as she continued to yell at me. I had enough.

This has gone too far.

I looked down at her, "Are you done yet?"

She gasped in disgust, perhaps at the fact that I had the courage to say something back. I saw her lift her right arm and make a fist.

Is she really about to try to punch me?

She sure was.

Engage ninja-mode.

Everything moved in slow motion – a real-life matrix scene. Right before her fist collided with my left eye, I snapped out of slow motion and reacted. My left hand quickly grabbed the wrist of her punching arm and shoved her to the ground.

Immediately, her name-calling ceased. She was down for the count.

Oh my gosh! Did that just happen?

It sure did.

Okay, step out of my awful college party for a moment and let's look at the big idea here.

What was I fighting this mean girl for? Well, partly for self-defense, but it all began because we were fighting for a man's heart.

Want to hear something crazy?

God is fighting that battle every day, the battle for your heart. It's an ugly one, full of bumps and bruises, but it's a ring God enters into for you. It's a battle He's willing to fight because that's how much He wants your heart.

God pursues you when you give him the cold shoulder. He goes to battle for you without you even knowing it. He goes before you to protect you, provide for you, and love you. He fights for you more than any knight in shining armor or a Prince Charming could ever dream of. He didn't just fight for you; He died for you.

So, the next time you feel torn between God and the world, know that He's hard at work fighting for you. Will you fight for Him? Will you take a stand for Him? Will you fight for intimacy with your Creator when a million distractions beg for your heart?

God fights for you, girl. He lost His life to save yours. Doesn't He deserve that you would live your life for Him?

TALK IT OUT

I want you take a peek in that boxing ring. I want you to
consider who is winning the battle and why. Who or what is
God's biggest opponent in the fight for your heart right now?
What in your life has such a handle on your heart that God
has to fight hard for it? Is it a person or relationship? A
disappointment you're dwelling on? Something else?

To find what's on the throne of your heart, consider where
you spend the majority of your time and money and where
you place the majority of your worries and energy. That's
where you'll find God's chief opponent for your heart. What
or who do *you* see sitting there?

"fear God" *↳ Be in awe of Him*

TRUTH SAYS...

Deuteronomy 5:9 describe God as a jealous God. He doesn't
want to share our heart with the things that we turn into gods.

Deuteronomy 20:4 reminds us that God fights for us. He
fights our battles against our enemies. Isn't it crazy to think
that the things we place so much of our hope in on earth can
actually be enemies to His kingdom when they begin to take
the place of God in our hearts?

THE BIG IDEA: JUST LIKE I DON'T WANT TO SHARE A BOY'S HEART, GOD DOESN'T WANT TO SHARE MY HEART

He craves our attention
desperate for time & attention

week 3: the no-text-back

Jeremiah 29:12
Psalm 17:6
Luke 18:1-8

"He still hasn't texted me back," my friend exclaimed as she curled her hair. "What could he possibly be doing? I should have never told him I liked him. Do you think it freaked him out? Does he still like me? I bet there's another girl."

I stopped applying my mascara and consoled her, "I wouldn't worry about it too much yet. It's only been one day."

She went on to tell me about why she was worried that he had lost interest. "Well, I know his ex-girlfriend was in town this weekend. I bet they hooked up!"

I did my best to comfort her but the reality is that she felt rejected, and none of my positive affirmations were really going to change that.

I'd be willing to bet you've had a conversation or two like this in your early adult years. If you've experienced rejection in any form, you know it doesn't feel good. It hurts to see our friends feel rejected almost as much as it hurts when we ourselves are rejected.

That's essentially why the no-text-back feels so icky. It's a subtle, indirect message that leaves us hanging and communicates the idea that we are more of an option than a priority.

It's an ugly feeling, isn't it?

He may simply be pre-occupied, or perhaps he may have found something or someone he likes more. Ugh. Worst feeling ever, right? Wouldn't you just rather be told directly that he's not interested? It sure would save a lot of headache!

A few weeks ago, I realized that I'm guilty of the no-text-back, too. I get preoccupied and wrapped up in things other than my relationship with God. I tend to treat Him more like a convenience or an option when something seemingly important or more interesting crosses my path.

Except, the difference between God and us is that when we are on the receiving end of the no-text-back, when we feel as though our prayers aren't answered in a timely manner, it's common for us to give up and move on. But when God is on the receiving end of our no-text-back, when we don't give Him the time of day, He just waits. He stays. He doesn't leave or give up on us. He's sitting by the phone, waiting for us to finally respond.

TALK IT OUT

Consider a time you've felt more like an option than a priority to someone. Have you been a victim of the no-text-back? How did it make you feel, and how did you react as a result?

Would you say you've treated God more like an option or a priority recently? Why?

What is it about prayer and communicating regularly with God that seems challenging to you?

TRUTH SAYS...

Jeremiah 29:12 is the Lord's reminder that when we do finally call on Him, He will listen. He will be there. He doesn't give up when we ignore Him. Man, I want to know a God like THAT! That makes me *want* to talk to Him!

Psalm 17:6 is another place in Scripture that points to God's faithfulness. He doesn't reject us when we reject Him. He hears our call and turns His ear toward us.

Luke 18:1-8 is a parable Jesus tells to encourage his disciples to pray and not give up. Prayer doesn't have to be incredibly formal, long, difficult, or boring. It is a tool given to us to communicate with God, invite Him into our days, and endure when we feel like giving up and walking away.

CHALLENGE:

For the next 7 days, identify one thing that is the chief competition in your heart for time with God each day. Maybe it's social media or the need to succeed or an obsessive relationship. Whatever it is, sacrifice 15 minutes of it each day or cut it out completely and replace it with prayer, meditation, fellowship, or time in the Word.

THE BIG IDEA: TEXT GOD BACK

week 4: the emotional turtle shell

Isaiah 2:22
Psalm 118:8
James 4:14

Not too long ago, I received an email from a reader. She explained how she felt like she had been living in an *emotional turtle shell* when it came to romantic relationships. Not that she was afraid of putting herself out there or meeting new guys, but the second it became more serious she wanted to run and hide.

She asked, "Do I have commitment issues? Maybe I'm afraid of being vulnerable."

If this sounds like you, you're not alone. I've personally experienced these feelings, too. I'd soak up all the attention a guy was willing to give, but I retreated to my turtle shell as soon as I felt like the light-hearted relationship would require me to invest too much time, energy, or emotion.

Looking back on that time as well as looking at God's Word, I think the root problem here is *fear*. Each and every situation is different, so the cause for our fear may be different. Perhaps it's fear of being hurt again, or fear of losing freedom, or fear of choosing the *wrong* person.

Every single one of those feelings is normal, worthy, and valid. The reality is that maybe the emotional turtle shell isn't a disease. Maybe it's a good thing. Maybe it's a way of guarding our heart. Maybe it's the Spirit working in us, signaling us: *NOPE! NOPE! NOT THE ONE!*

I believe that if we really had peace about starting a relationship, we would hold God's hand and take a leap of faith regardless of the temptation to be afraid.

But consider this: what is fear? Joseph Murphy said, "Fear is *faith* in the wrong thing."[1]

When we experience feelings of fear regarding a potential significant other, we are essentially trying to put our faith in that person – faith that they will love us how we need to be loved, give us the space we need, faith that they won't hurt us, etc.

If we put our faith in anything other than God, we're going to make that other thing our god. A god that cannot fulfill our deepest needs. Of course we feel fear! Our inmost being knows that that is an impossible responsibility for another person!

So, if you're constantly retreating back to your turtle shell, afraid of being let down or committing to something or someone that could let you down, look at where you're placing your faith.

Fear, even of heartbreak, isn't so bad when we place our faith in God over a guy.

TALK IT OUT

What gives you the most anxiety or fear when it comes to guys and/or dating?

What about the dating scene has encouraged or discouraged you?

Whether or not you've started a personal relationship with God, what holds you back from completely trusting Him with your heart?

TRUTH SAYS...

Isaiah 2:22 and Psalm 118:8 advise us that it is best to put our trust in the Lord rather than to place our faith in humans.

James 4:14 is a humbling truth. It states the reality of our life: our life is a mist and we are not guaranteed tomorrow. When we place more energy in worrying about what *could* happen tomorrow, we fail to trust God *today*.

THE BIG IDEA: FEAR IS PUTTING FAITH IN THE WRONG THING

It's better to take refuge in the Lord than to trust a man.

It's better to take refuge in the Lord than to trust in princes

week 5: clean on the inside, clean on the outside

1 Corinthians 10:12-14
Psalm 51:10
Ephesians 5:7-14
Romans 2:4
Romans 3:23
Romans 6:7

I don't wash my car often, but when I do I'm sure to clear off every stitch of dirt. When I'm finished, the old girl is super shiny and I feel like a rock star driving around town. It looks good, right? It looks clean and perfect... from the outside.

What my fellow motorists don't see is the inside of my car. More than likely, it needs to be vacuumed and there's probably an old Starbucks cup (or five) rolling around the floor.

I'm sharing this little insight into my car because I think it paints a strong picture of the way we look at the idea of purity. I think it's something we need to be more real and honest about, because everybody struggles with purity, regardless of his or her sexual activity.

This may be TMI, but I struggled with masturbation (awkward enough for ya?) for several years as a teenager. By the time I realized that's what it was—and that it was a sin—it had already become an ugly habit.

On the outside I kept a shiny, clean reputation, but on the inside I felt so dirty and stuck until I finally began to talk about it. At the time, it was really hard but God allowed me to walk through that struggle and find freedom from it so that I can give the hope message to others who may be secretly struggling with any form of sexual sin.

I'm not ashamed to talk about that time in my adolescent life because I think sexual sin and struggle has far too many women in bondage. But the reality is that there's no way to find freedom from it without opening up the doors of our hearts, exposing it to the light, and talking about it.

If your confidence rests in Christ, the judgmental glares you may get have no hold on your heart, and you have the power to do that. Wherever you are on the purity scale, please realize that you're not hopeless and that grace hasn't run out for you when you think it has. Although I don't know the specifics of your struggle, I do know that you are a daughter of God and that you're no worse or better than His other daughters.

Because when you open the doors of the car, when you look into the heart of the matter, there's dust and impurities in all of us. There is more than sexual purity.

There is such thing as emotional purity, too. Are we guarding our hearts and protecting our minds? See? It's not just about what so-and-so did with that guy.

This can't be a comparison thing, nor can it be a self-righteous thing. The concept of sexual purity can almost become an idol when we begin to make it about our behavior record. God doesn't like promiscuity, but He also doesn't like pride. Both of these separate our hearts from His true, good, and real love.

But the good news is that all things are redeemable. This has to be a full dependence and reliance kind of thing. We can't rely on our own car washing abilities to purify us from the inside out.

Why? Because eventually we'll drive through a mud puddle and what really matters is the inside, the heart of the matter. In other words, we can't be pure on our own.

Worry less about another girl's shine and more about letting God strengthen you by vacuuming out the shame and struggle that are cluttering your heart.

Open the door, invite Him in, and let Him work from the inside out.

TALK IT OUT

What impurities have you been wrestling with in your life? They can be internal and spiritual or external and sexual. Be honest; this is a safe place.

Have you confessed these to God? If not, you have freedom to share it here now and find freedom. This is a safe place and a judgment free zone.

TRUTH SAYS…

1 Corinthians 10:12-14 is packed with two powerful truths for when something gets really, really, really, really, really (did I say really?) hard. The first is that you're not alone; others have faced what you're facing. You're also not doomed. God knows your temptation and He will give you a way out and the strength to overcome it.

Psalm 51:10 reminds us that we cannot create our own pure heart. It's an action of God that He will do when we cry out for help.

Ephesians 5:7-14 tells us that crying out for help also requires vulnerability and humility. If we don't trust the Lord enough to expose our sin and brokenness, then we don't trust Him enough to free us from it. Shame has a way of shackling our hearts and enslaving us to hiding our sin butut truth tells us that true freedom is found in vulnerability and repentance. When our confidence rests in Christ, we can expose our weakness and the enemy has no hold on us then.

Romans 2:4 is a reminder that God's kindness is intended to lead us to repentance. His love and mercy are so great that it ought to compel our hearts to confess our shortcomings and impurities honestly to find freedom. Who wouldn't want freedom?

Romans 3:23 serves as a powerful reminder to not compare our level of purity to a sister's, because all have sinned and fallen short of the glory of God. We can only look to Jesus.

Romans 6:7 is the powerful truth that grace is not cheap. God is willing and able to cleanse us from the inside out, but we can't take that for granted; we can't go on carelessly expecting God to just fix it. We need to be intentional about inviting Him into our brokenness and temptation to overcome it. A heart change always comes before a behavior change. When you let Him change your heart from the inside out, you will be better equipped to resist behaviors that are damaging.

THE BIG IDEA: VULNERABILITY = FREEDOM

GROUP CHALLENGE: Lift each girl's specific struggle in prayer.

week 6: let yourself be loved

Romans 5:8
1 John 4:9-11
John 4:1-26
Hosea 2:14-19

In college, my mom called me frequently. When I was preoccupied with my friends, busy with my schoolwork, or just not in the mood for a long conversation, I often sent her call to voicemail.

Don't get me wrong, I love my mom. I honor her and trust her guidance. But I often fail to let myself really feel her love and hear her voice. I often push her desire to get to know me more to the back burner, probably because in the back of my mind I know she will always be there.

I think walking with God can feel very similar. Sometimes we make it out to be more like a burden than beautiful.

Here's what I mean. We honor God and trust Him as the all-powerful and all-knowing King. We fear Him and believe in His world-making, universe designing power. But what about the compassionate God? The One who died to win us, the God who is crazy jealous, the Father who pursues our hearts with reckless abandon. Do we really know Him? Or is it too hard for us to accept that a God so big could notice and love a heart as small as our own?

We need to realize that He's been calling and leaving voicemails, relentlessly pursuing our hearts since day one. He wants us to get to know Him, not because He needs us but because He knows how desperately we need Him: His character, His wild love, and His care for us that runs deeper than the sea. Otherwise, we are going to look for that love in every other thing this world has to offer.

Maybe you're the girl that has never dated anyone, or that only got asked to a dance once, or has been called a prude for waiting until marriage. Or maybe you're the girl that that scoffs at the idea of waiting until marriage. Maybe you're sitting on a bucket full of shame after that one night, or maybe you feel uncomfortable when any guy looks at you, or you're afraid of being lonely forever.

Regardless of which category you fall under, the Lord will lead you to someone whose love mirrors His love, even if that's to His arms alone.

If you're having a hard time really knowing and loving God in college, if the world around you makes you believe that knowing God is a chore, stop trying to love God and let Him love you. Let yourself feel His love first. Let yourself listen to the voicemails that He's left for you in His Word and in the creation of His world.

You are called into a beautiful love story, a wild adventure, and an incredible purpose right now. But first, you've gotta pick up the phone.

TALK IT OUT

Have you gotten to know God's love for you? Or does He still feel like a far off, holy, big and mighty God that you haven't been able to experience?

Describe a time that you really felt God's love in your life.

Consider a time you doubted God's love for you. What makes it hard for you to believe that God wants you to walk with Him and communicate with Him – even now, in college, when life demands so much of you?

TRUTH SAYS...

Romans 5:8 tells us that even while we rejected God, even when we sent Him to voicemail, His love still pursued us. Even as sinners – those who hurt, offend, and neglect God – Christ still died for us so that we could be united to God. God knows how much we need to be near Him, hear from Him, and experience His love.

1 John 4:9-11 reminds us that we haven't loved God but He has loved us, enough to send His Son to die on our behalf so that we might live. This is love. This is wild, compassionate, chasing our hearts down love. Has it won you over yet?

John 4:1-26 is the story of the woman at the well. Jesus went out of His way to speak to her, to love her enough to show her who He was, and to open her eyes to eternal life. Look at verses 16-18. Jesus already knew that the woman didn't actually have a husband, but He requests that she bring her husband in order to help her understand what this "living water" that He was referring to really is. Tim Keller teaches a great sermon on this passage. In essence, he teaches that when she shares that she has no husband and He reveals that He knows she has in fact had five men, or husbands, He is showing her the truth that she has have been seeking fulfillment outside Him, the Living Water. She was looking for the living water in the wrong place—in men—which is why she's had so many husbands. In this passage, Jesus reveals that man will not satisfy a thirsty heart like He can, and therefore she will always be thirsty again. Jesus reveals that the only way she can quench the thirst in her heart is with the living water that flows only from Him.[2]

Hosea 2:14-19 describes God's pursuit of us. He wants us to experience the love He has for us, a love even more intimate and true than that of a groom to a bride on earth. The love He pursues us with is steadfast, tender, and sacrificial. The closest thing it mirrors on this earth is the love between a husband and a wife, without sin's power.

THE BIG IDEA: LET GOD LOVE YOU LIKE YOU NEED TO BE LOVED

Identity Crisis:

Rediscovering and Reclaiming Who We REALLY Are

Hey girlfriend!

Have you ever seen that movie _Identity Thief_ with Melissa McCarthy? If not, I highly recommend it.

I watched it a few months ago and I found myself laughing so hard that I snorted out loud (embarrassing). I was both humored and entertained by the story and touches of comedy throughout movie. If you haven't seen it, a man gets his identity stolen and the thief, Diana, played by Melissa McCarthy, is an absolutely hilarious little villain. The victim experiences all sorts of pain as a result of Diana's recklessness.

As I thought about the movie later on, I realized how much the grief our hearts experience when our true identity as daughters of God is snatched from us is like the victim's in the movie.

My hope behind this study is to help you reclaim your identity in the middle of the four years that the world tries to slap all sorts of labels and identities on you that you were never meant to wear.

So, if you're trying to sift through who you are or if you're hoping to experience what it's really like to be a daughter of the Lord God, we've got a lot to work through together in three short weeks.

Grab a bucket of popcorn and press play.

Xox,

jordan lee

For more, follow me online!
Facebook: **Jordan Lee**
Instagram: @**soulscripts**
www.thesoulscripts.com

week 1: you are not yesterday

Isaiah 43:18-19
Philippians 3:13-14
Romans 6:6

I hear a lot of football lingo in my house. When my husband talks with his agent, teammates, or friends on the phone, I hear all sorts of sports jabber. Something I've heard him talk about a lot is the importance of a "next play mentality."

I recently asked him about the whole "next play mentality" concept and he explained it to me like this:

"The most successful players in the NFL, or really any professional sport, have a *next play mentality*. When they make a mistake or fail in some way, they are able to quickly flush the mistake from their mind and look forward to the next play. Those are the ones who rise above the mistake and succeed. The last play doesn't dictate the next play. But the players who make a mistake and dwell on it, the ones who can't move past it mentally or emotionally, implode. They collapse in on themselves, and instead of having one bad play it will turn into several bad plays, which can quickly end their career."

The concept was simple yet profound. The weight it held for players in a football game is the same weight it holds for people in the game of life. We have the choice to decide if we are going to let our yesterday dictate our today.

When we dwell on our past mistakes, it's very difficult to embrace our identity as a new creation in Christ. We are essentially rejecting the identity shift we are invited into when we choose Christ as our Savior – the identity shift that gives us power over all earthly things.

If you're dwelling on guilt you've carried, mistakes you've made, or sins you're having trouble shaking, remember the importance of a next play mentality. When you stop focusing on the last play and look ahead to the next, you are best able to rise above the enemy's attempts to collapse the hope in your heart.

It's not about what you've done, but what Jesus has done on the cross. He rose above all sin and death – past, present, and future. He's reaching His hand out and daring you to get up off the floor of regret, guilt, shame, fear, and sadness. He's challenging you to stand up and reclaim your true identity.

Stop dwelling on the last play. Get up. Eyes on the prize. Next play.

You are not your past, you are not your mistakes, and you are not yesterday.

TALK IT OUT

Is there something in your past, even as recent as a few minutes ago, that is holding you back from living out or reclaiming your true identity as a daughter of God? Share what that is.

What in your life do you believe weighs you down or limits you from living out your God-given potential?

TRUTH SAYS...

Isaiah 43:18-19 is a piece of Isaiah's writings to the children of Israel after a rough period of their history. In this passage, they are in captivity and have lost everything. These verses were originally written to motivate God's chosen nation of Israel to fix their focus on the new things God is doing in their lives and to look ahead, rather than dwell on the past and look behind. But we can use them for the same purposes in our lives today. In order to move on to the new creation you are in Christ, you cannot allow your past mistakes or shortcomings to enslave your heart or mind.

Philippians 3:13-14 describes the process of growth as a Christian. The Christian life is often described as a race. We're not in the race because of our own effort, but because we agreed when Jesus took our hand and said, "Hey girl, run with Me!" In this passage, Paul shows us that developing a personal relationship with Jesus is the prize, and that in order to win the prize, we've got to have the right attitude, a "next play mentality." We can't win a race and press on toward the prize if we are constantly looking back. If eternity with Jesus is the prize at the finish line, how can we fix our eyes on Him if we are constantly looking back, away from Him, to the starting line that we came from?

Romans 6:6 reminds us that because of what Jesus did, we are no longer slaves to sin. We are not slaves to the past but set free from it because Christ conquered it once and for all on our behalf. Shake off the chains you've put on yourself and keep running forward with your eyes ahead.

THE BIG IDEA: GET UP, EYES ON THE PRIZE, NEXT PLAY

week 2: who you are is not what you do

Jeremiah 1:5
John 1:12
Ephesians 1:5
Colossians 3:1-13

In high school, I discovered I had an average ability for scoring three pointers in basketball. Again, I said average. But at the time I thought I was a total rock star for having a 50% shooting average.

Each time I scored, my stomach did giddy flip-flops while my face remained focused and intense. On the outside, I remained cool, calm, and collected because I'd been told it's important to "act like you've been there before."

Psh, yeah, no big deal. I do this all the time...

I played it off cool but what I *really* wanted to do was squeal and jump up and down. I'd occasionally glance over at my coach to see if he noticed.

Did you see that, Coach? I did something good! I did something good! I'm a good basketball player!

After a good game, I thrived on high fives from teammates, coaches, and classmates. After a not-so-good, low-scoring game for me, I sulked in frustration as I watched my teammates receive those high fives. I questioned my ability, my skill, and my worth in the game.

133

I started off my senior season strong. I lived for the high fives and *way to go's* I'd get after each game. Midway through the season, I lost it. I lost my touch. Each attempt I made at a three pointer was a brick or an air ball. I wasn't sure how to explain it. My coaches were stumped. By the time playoffs rolled around, I was benched.

We won a championship, but I never saw the floor. It didn't matter that my teammates had won, because inside, I was defeated.

I fought back tears as the girls celebrated around me. I didn't understand why I didn't even get a chance. My feelings in that moment captured the reality of my situation: my basketball performance had become the thing I used to measure my worth, and that night I felt worthless to my team. They didn't need me. I didn't make a difference. I didn't have the purpose I thought I did. I was useless.

When I hung up my basketball shoes and started college, my good grades became to me what basketball had been to me in high school – a measure of my worth, and it therefore defined who I was. It was no longer about being a good basketball player but about being good student, instead of resting in the Truth that above all else I was a daughter of God.

The pressure I put on myself to perform well and to be a good student consumed my heart. Eventually it became the measurement of my entire value.

During my junior year, I hit my breaking point. On an evening in the spring, I found myself drowning in so many papers, projects, and study guides that I thought I might go under for good and lose my identity as a good student.

It was as if my vision had grown so clouded with everything I had to do that I lost who I was. Maybe you've reached this point before, or maybe you're feeling it now.

Something inside of me snapped and I cried out to God, "WHO THE HECK AM I?!"

I listened for a moment, waiting for a comforting voice to say something like, "You're a good student. You're a friend. You're a hard worker. You're a leader. A winner..."

But I didn't hear that. I didn't receive anything.

I asked again, "WHO AM I, GOD?!"

One word was placed on my heart. A word I hadn't prepared for. A response I wasn't looking for but so desperately needed.

Do you want to know what it was?

MINE.

All the other titles and accomplishments I had placed next to my name faded into the background of my mind and vanished like a mist.

In that moment, I realized that who I am has nothing to do with what I do but everything with who God is.

Let me say it again: *Who you are is **not** what you do.*

Work hard. Dream big. Set goals. But in the midst of all your doing and dreaming, remember that your identity isn't measured by what you do. It's established in what Jesus has done, is doing, and will do – for you.

You are His. You are one with Him. Everything else is just extra.

TALK IT OUT

What earthly currencies have you been measuring your worth by? Grades? Followers? People's opinions? Something else?

What in your life do you believe limits you from living out your true identity as God's chosen, beloved, daughter?

TRUTH SAYS...

Jeremiah 1:5 says that even before we are even a thought, before we become a person with a soul, and before we know who we are, God knows us deeply and personally. He held our hearts before they ever existed.

John 1:12 reminds us of our true identity. When our life on earth ends, we are not identified as students. We are not identified as athletes. We are not identified as friends or professionals or anything other than children of God.

Ephesians 1:5 tells us that we have been set apart for adoption as children of God through Jesus Christ. God does not fail to remind us of our familial status and identity in His kingdom. He knows to whom we belong when we forget, and He will never fail to remind us if we ask.

Colossians 3:1-3 tells us to set our mind on things above, not on things of earth. Our life, our entire identity and worth, is now hidden with Christ, not in what we do here on earth.

THE BIG IDEA: WHO I AM IS NOT WHAT I DO

week 3: Tune into the truth about you

Genesis 1:27
Psalm 139:14
Romans 15:7

Ever heard of a Walkman?

Before iPods and iPhones and all the other rad music playing devices came out, there was the Walkman. A Walkman was a little device with headphones that played music on a CD (or even cassette tapes!) back in the day.

I often rocked out to my little Walkman in my purple childhood bedroom before school. I remember listening to the music, dancing shamelessly on my bed, and clinging to every word. I always put my favorite songs on repeat.

As I look back at those memories, I'm reminded that sometimes it's as if we have a CD playing on repeat in our heads – little voices feeding us lines that we cling to.

But I think somewhere along the way, we stop dancing. When life gets hard, when someone judges us, or when something makes us feel small, the enemy takes that weak moment as an opportunity to scratch the CD in our heads.

Suddenly, the lines in the song we march to the beat of are no longer just lines but LIES.

When we face disappointment or failure, it says things like:
You're not nearly as talented as your friends.
Why try?

You're nothing special.

When we add something that was intended to be funny to a conversation and no one laughs, it plays:
Did you really just say that? You're not funny.

When we aren't invited, it sings:
You're not fun. People don't like your personality.

The song continues to play over and over, convincing us of an identity we were never meant to have, but we listen anyway. We cling to every word and *believe* every sentence without even realizing it.

However, if we press pause on the lies playing in our head and swap out the CD for God's truth about us, we're going to hear a different tune, a sweeter melody, and a better beat.

If the enemy has snatched the tunes of truth out of your head and traded it for lines and lyrics of lies, don't forget you have the power to get it back. God has given us the ultimate mix tape in His Word. If what you're believing about yourself doesn't line up with who HE says that you are in His Word, *then it's a lie.*

His Word says, "Yes, you are broken and messy, but you're not stuck there. You are redeemed and loved – not for your glory, but God's."

So, you might as well press pause on the junk, eject that CD, tune in, and listen to what your Father says about you.

TALK IT OUT

What is the biggest lie about your identity that you have to fight?

When do you hear or believe the scratched CD, or the enemy's lie about your identity, the most?

TRUTH SAYS...

Genesis 1:27 says that we are made in the image and likeness of God.

Psalm 139:14 reminds us that we have been intentionally and intricately designed, that we are fearfully and wonderfully made, not for our glory but His. The beauty of who we are reflects the beauty of God because we are made *by* Him *in* His image. It is all FOR Him. Our identity is in who He is.

Romans 15:7 tells us that we are to accept one another because we have been accepted by Christ. A crucial part of our identity is that we have been accepted as fellow heirs to the Kingdom.

THE BIG IDEA: YOUR TRUE IDENTITY DOES NOT REFLECT WHO THE WORLD SAYS YOU ARE BUT WHO GOD SAYS THAT *HE* IS

The Sisterhood:

Four Weeks on Friendship & Fitting In

Hey girlfriend!

I've written a study on friendship because I believe that strong, honest friendship is one of the sweetest gifts life has to offer. But I also know it can be one of the most frustrating things, too.

For a long time, I wanted a lot of friends. I longed to be in a group but always ended up a floater. Then, I tried having just one or two friends and keeping them all to myself. I held them so close I nearly suffocated them and our friendship suffered for it.

Over the course of my four years in college, I learned a lot about the realities of friendship and how God fits into that equation.

Although I'm no expert and I don't know what your friendship or social life looks like, I know that this study pertains to you in one way or another. Perhaps you've never had a problem making friends but struggle keeping them. Or the thought of introducing yourself to someone new scares the socks right off you. Or maybe you're wondering if your friends *really* know you. Maybe you're looking for something *more* than just friends. Maybe you're looking for sisters.

Whatever your social situation currently is, I think it's worth talking about and inviting Jesus into, because friendship is hard, FOMO is real, and feeling left out really stinks.

So, let's talk about it. We all come from different places, have different testimonies, and share different experiences when it comes to friendship. But I hope that at the end of this, we will find some common ground and be encouraged in one simple truth: we are designed for real, true, lasting friendship. Together, we're going to discover just how to attain it.

Xox,

jordan lee

For more, follow me online!
Facebook: **Jordan Lee**
Instagram: **@soulscripts**
www.thesoulscripts.com

week 1: a place to belong

Isaiah 43:1
Romans 8:15
1 John 4:4

"I will never join a sorority," I told my mom as she helped me pack for college.

"Okay, that's fine. You don't have to do anything you don't want to do," she responded.

One year later, I found myself running late the first morning of recruitment. I fixed my mascara, grabbed my schedule, and darted across the meadow to the house where my first round took place. I stood in line with nearly one hundred other girls, all of us looking around at each other, comparing our makeup and outfits, wondering how we size up.

What am I doing here? I remember thinking.

Before I knew it, the doors swung open, girls started cheering, and we were herded inside.

As I went through the recruitment process as a PNM (Potential New Member), I carried on countless conversations with different sorority women as they graded me on my conversation skills, humor, involvement, presentation, academics, and more. I felt the same feelings every other PNM felt that week:
What do they think of me?
Did I say something wrong?
Why did that house drop me?
Maybe I'm not as fun and flirty as the other girls.

I just wanted what every other girl wanted: a place to belong. I wanted to find a good group of likeminded girls in the midst of a giant campus. I wanted to find my *home*.

But finding a place to belong, a group of sisters, and a home seemed much more difficult than I had imagined. It required me to put on my very best face and my very best behavior. It required me to filter my true beliefs, say the appropriate thing, and smile.

Whether or not you've ever gone through sorority recruitment, I'm certain that you've not only longed for a place to belong but also wondered if you measure up to the women around you who seem to have no problem finding their place.

Finding, building, and maintaining meaningful friendships can be really hard. We all know it's incredibly difficult for women to avoid comparison and competition, even with their closest friends. Sometimes, we wonder if we really have a place to belong – a place to call home.

Recruitment came to a close on bid day. I felt a huge sigh of relief when I received a bid – it was essentially my certificate that said, "Congratulations. You made it. You proved yourself worthy and we approve of you. You fit in somewhere. Here's your proof. Come move in here."

I was over the moon. I did it!

Okay, now I invite you to step out of recruitment for a moment. If you've been searching for a place to belong, constantly comparing yourself and trying to prove yourself (or if you're simply trying to maintain the place you belong), we need to look at this through a different lens.

Although sometimes finding a place to call home on this earth can be really hard, don't forget that any home you manage to find on this planet is temporary. It's not a recruitment process in God's kingdom.

We don't have to earn a bid. He's given us direct access to our eternal address because of His Son. The day we accept Him as our Savior and make Him the Lord of our life, there's nothing we have to prove anymore. We don't have to prove ourselves with our accomplishments, our presentation, our academics, or our popularity.

He's given us a place to belong, a circle of eternal friendships, and a home in His kingdom. It's not something we can earn, and it's completely backwards compared to every other process of getting into something on earth. I guess that's why He calls it grace.

Whatever your status is here on earth, if you wear letters on your chest and have the greatest BFF's in the whole wide world or if you feel like you're going through recruitment just and trying to find a place to belong, don't forget where or to Whom you *truly* belong. Don't forget in THAT house, in God's house, you are fully known and fully loved at your best AND at your worst. It's a place where your brokenness is welcome; not only is it welcome – it's redeemed.

TALK IT OUT

Regardless of whether or not you belong to a social group, sorority, or other circle, look inside your heart. What about building or maintaining meaningful friendship has been challenging for you?

Do you compare yourself to your friends or feel jealous of the girls around you?

Have you ever felt excluded, uninvited, left out, or alone, even within your circle of friends?
If you're in a group study, share that experience with the girls around you.
If you're studying individually, write it down and pray through it.

TRUTH SAYS...

Isaiah 43:1 is God's words sharing the encouraging truth that He knows us fully, calls us by name, and claims us as His own. We belong with and to God despite our broken, imperfect pieces.

Romans 8:15 reminds us of our adoption as God's daughters. He has welcomed us in. He has opened the door to all of us. When we think we don't belong, we have the invitation to look around and see our sisters, but more importantly to look up and see our Abba Father.

1 John 4:4 says that when we are judged or graded on our appearance, presentation, accomplishments, etc. by people of earth, that we have victory over people's opinions because the Spirit who lives in us is greater than that which is in the

world. We cannot be defeated and competition is unnecessary; we are already victorious in the one way that counts. #winning

THE BIG IDEA: YOU BELONG AND HAVE AN ETERNAL HOME

week 2: expired

Proverbs 18:24
Proverbs 27:17
John 15:13-15

One time I called my mom in tears as I blurted out these words: "I'M LIKE A GALLON OF MILK WITH AN EXPIRATION DATE!"

After a sweet chuckle on the other line and a few minutes of sobbing, I was able to explain my frustration with friendships.

I felt like as soon as I would grow close to a friend, we would grow apart. Or she would find other, cooler, more fun friends and suddenly vibes were weird and I couldn't figure out if something was wrong with me or if I did something to screw up another friendship. I would look online and see pictures of cliques and feel even more isolated.

I'd go to parties, bee-bop to the music and watch groups of girls take selfies. Or I'd be asked to take a picture of them only to see it on Facebook the next day WITHOUT a photo cred.

UGH. RUDE, RIGHT?

I'm being dramatic but I have a point.

There have been times in my life that I truly believed that true, lifelong friendship was hopeless. I wondered if I had unrealistic expectations or if I just wasn't someone people could relate to. I felt as though my friendships were constantly changing, and I longed for consistency. I had a lot of good friends over the years but I wanted something more. I just couldn't put my finger on what that *more* was.

Over time, I learned that I wasn't alone in these feelings. The more I shared my frustration, the more I learned that *most* women actually feel insecure when it comes to their friendships.

No way! I never would have guessed!

And the craziest part? They shared that they never would have guessed I struggled with those feelings, too.

Isn't it crazy what a little honesty can do for our hearts? I didn't feel so alone anymore, and I gained a renewed sense of hope *and* understanding of the girls around me. I had to strip my heart of any bitterness I had been harboring and start over by pursuing friendships with a whole new approach.

Want to know what it was?

I realized I had to stop making friendships about *me*. I had to stop expecting them to fill the hole in my heart. When I did that, I was going to be let down 100% of the time. Any friendships I share on this earth have to be the direct result of my friendship with Jesus – not a replacement for it. When my friendships began to be motivated by a desire to include others in that friendship with Him, my frustration with the flaws of friendship faded.

So, if you wonder if something is wrong with you because you're having trouble keeping strong female friendships, I just want to remind you to look at what you're fixated on. Do you look at friendship as a gift, or do you look at friends as a god?

I think with social media and all the displays of what the world tells us friendship looks like, it's incredibly easy to turn the idea of friendship into a god, or an idol, in our lives. Friendship is a gift but it is not God.

Just like we can settle for a guy when we feel lonely, I believe it's possible to also settle for friends that don't truly sharpen or love us when we feel lonely. Sometimes it's okay for certain relationships to expire; sometimes it's the very best thing for us.

Because you know what? All things are redeemable. At the end of the day, you are not alone. He knows we need community and He will deliver whom you need, right when you need them, to stand by you in the rain. Through it all, He never leaves your side.

So, keep on keepin' on, because the moment you realize that God has given you the greatest Friend in His Son, you'll see that you're NOT a gallon of milk, but a gal loved by the Messiah.

That's *not* a friendship that has an expiration date.

TALK IT OUT

Have you ever had a relationship with a friend expire? In other words, have you ever grown apart from or ended a friendship with someone? How did that experience make you feel?

What is your biggest struggle when it comes to friendship? Do you ever feel like you're the only one who struggles with girl friendships?

When you feel lonely, do you first talk to your friends or do you talk to Jesus?

Do you ever struggle to grow in friendship with Jesus? Is it difficult for you to see Him as both Lord and friend?

TRUTH SAYS...

Proverbs 18:24 is a nugget of wisdom that urges us to focus on quality over quantity. It is incredibly difficult to build AND keep a lot of friendships for any extended length of time. Instead, it's wise to invest in a small circle and really nurture those relationships.

Proverbs 27:17 tells us that iron sharpens iron. Friendship is a good thing. It is a gift that, if used properly, can sharpen and strengthen us.

John 15:13-15 are the words of Jesus. He tells us the profound truth that there is no greater love than the one who lays down his life for a friend. *He did that for you and me.* He calls us friends and is serious about us and about our friendship.

THE BIG IDEA: EARTHLY FRIENDSHIP HAS TO
BE THE **RESULT** OF FRIENDSHIP WITH JESUS,
NOT A REPLACEMENT FOR IT

week 3: house-divided

Malachi 2:10
1 Peter 3:8
Romans 12:4-6
Romans 12:16

During my time in Greek life, I heard all the Greek gossip and often noticed the division between the communities as a whole. I remember seeing girls walk past each other, look at each other, and quietly make judgments based on the letters the other girl wore on her shirt.

I would hear comments on the bus:
Did you hear that (insert sorority house here) is on probation?
Those girls are so easy.
*That frat paired with **that sorority**?!*

Maybe you've experience the Greek life gossip. Maybe you've never set foot in a Greek house. Either way, I'm sure you've experienced the division that comparison and competition causes.

Women are competitive creatures. Comparison fuels the competition.

But what is comparison?

Comparison is the catalyst for crumbling any sense of community.

If you've experienced division within your friendship circle or in the community you are part of (sorority, club, or even ministry group), consider the deeper issue.

Comparison crumbles community and is fueled by a certain type of petroleum: pride.

But community that is *built by compassion* and unity is *fueled by humility.*

Why? Because when compassion and humility are at work, we are capable of opening up and linking arms, even when it compromises our own ability to be the best or to stand out. It requires a sacrifice, but it's a worthy one because the cost of comparison is isolation. Who really wants to be isolated? It's a painful place.

I get it. No one wants to be the less successful, not-as-pretty friend. But maybe if we stop looking out and start looking up, we would see we're all on the same level when we compare ourselves to God. Sometimes, unity has to be prompted by one person, willing to reach outside of herself, get uncomfortable, and be vulnerable with her own imperfections.

So, if you're feeling isolated, consider this: If we took off our earthly glasses and replaced them with eternal glasses, then our sister's better grade, guy, Greek house, or social circle would be something to celebrate instead of scowl at.

TALK IT OUT

Look inside your heart and at your community with God and His people. Are you ruled by compassion or comparison?

How has comparison affected your girl friendships?

How have you experienced division within your social groups? A sorority, ministry, church group, classroom project, etc.

TRUTH SAYS...

Malachi 2:10 is an Old Testament truth that reminds us of our true status. When we get too busy comparing our earthly popularity and performance, we forget our eternal status. We are all united as daughters; we are siblings on the same playing field, loved and created by the same God. True brotherly (or sisterly) love often beckons us to sacrifice our own status for the sake of unity.

1 Peter 3:8 urges us to choose compassion and humility. While it is sometimes difficult to be like-minded, we ought not to let our differences divide us in the church, but instead extend a compassionate and humble hand.

Romans 12:4-6 discusses the importance of our different gifts. It is useless to compare the function of the foot to the hand because they are designed to do different things, and neither is more important than the other. Likewise, it is useless to compare our gifts, abilities, and appearance to that of a friend because we are designed to do different things, and neither is more important than the other.

Romans 12:16 reminds us to shut off the pipe that's pumping pride into our hearts and instead keep our hearts humble with compassion and outreach. When we don't feel like we have a strong group of friends or a united community, we have the choice to let our pride make us arrogant and angry or to let Christ create in us compassion and humility.

THE BIG IDEA: COMPASSION > COMPARISON

week 4. community > company

Matthew 18:20
Hebrews 10:24-25
1 John 4:11

In high school, I never really fit into a group. I had friends, but they were all part of *other* groups; groups that I wasn't in.

For a while, I enjoyed having a diverse group of friends, but over time I began to resent it. I hated that despite how close we were, if other group events were happening, I was left alone on a Friday night.

By the time I walked into my freshman year of college, I was ready for a group of my own! I felt that I had deserved it. I immediately surrounded myself with anyone who was nice to me. I really didn't even get to know them, to be honest. I just wanted to be surrounded by friends. I wanted to know that I had somewhere to go and someone to go with on Friday night. I craved their company.

As my understanding of friendship and relationships matured over the four years I spent at IU, I began to realize that it wasn't company that I craved; it was *community*.

Not until my senior year did I realize that there was a difference.

Company is not the same as community. Real community, the kind of community our hearts were designed for, isn't necessarily just about keeping each other company.

159

Company often masks itself as community – people to pass the time with, laugh with, and make memories with. And there's nothing wrong with that.

But the problem with company is that it doesn't really know you. It can't love you through your brokenness. It wants to see your smile but it doesn't know how to break through your barriers and listen to your heart.

If you're feeling unsatisfied, disappointed, discouraged, or alone even when surrounded by your group of friends, please realize that you are not alone. You were created for relationship by a Triune God who is, by nature, relationship. Because of that, you are invited to step into that relationship, to experience true community, and to link arms with believers in true fellowship. But there's a catch: you're going to have to be fully known – even the worst parts of you. But I promise that unlike company, true community will love you anyway.

TALK IT OUT

Consider if you've been seeking company or community.

Do you feel as though the people you surround yourself with *really* know you? What can you do to help them know you more, and for you to know them more also?

Does the group that you spend the most time with invest in you, encourage you, and sharpen you? Or do you feel as though you are a burden or have to act a certain way to fit in? What can you do to be more encouraged by those you hang out with, and to encourage them more?

TRUTH SAYS...

Matthew 18:20 points to the truth about community. When we gather together in God's name, He is present there. Godly community includes God.

Hebrews 10:24-25 highlights a key characteristic of community: encouragement. If your group is spurring each other on to love and goodness, you've found community. If your group is dragging you down or leaving you discouraged, it is likely that you've merely found company.

1 John 4:11 tells us that we have the ability to love only because we have first been loved by God. God created love – agape (sacrificial) love. When we step into community with God and His people, the defining factor must be *love* – genuine, self-sacrificing love.

THE BIG IDEA: GODLY COMMUNITY BEATS GOOD COMPANY

Limitless:

Let's Leave a Legacy

Hey girlfriend!

I've written this study because I believe YOU can leave a legacy for Christ.

Even if you are graduating in just a few short months, don't let the enemy tell you it's too late. Your legacy doesn't have to be big or famous. Actually, it likely will be humble and quiet and start in the hearts of just a few girls you invest in.

I can't help but think that this is how it should be because if we look at the way Jesus built His church. He wasn't interested in marketing Himself to the masses, nor was He interested in being everyone's best friend. He intentionally invested in a small group of men, who then invested in a few more, who then invested in a few more. The foundation of the greatest legacy of all time was laid.

If you're anything like I used to be, you may believe that you don't have much to offer the world. You may ask questions like, *how can I possibly leave a legacy?*

You know, I think it's really easy to assume we aren't cut out for Kingdom work. Perhaps you're really new to the whole Christian life thing. Maybe you're feeling really distant from God or down on yourself. It's incredibly easy to doubt our abilities. It's actually incredibly valid to doubt our abilities. We really aren't capable of all that much on our own. Praise God for His help, right?

Even if you are new to your faith or to a relationship with Jesus, you still have the power and the responsibility to pour the love message of the good news into those around you. It's not about how worthy you feel but how willing you are. It's not about your effort but your obedience.

Before you believe that this study doesn't apply to you, think again. Grab your slippers, maybe even some coffee, and snuggle into this one with me.

Because leaving a legacy for Christ isn't just a call; it's a command. With a little bit of coffee and whole lot of Jesus, you can do it, too.

Xox,

jordan lee

For more, follow me online!
Facebook: **Jordan Lee**
Instagram: **@soulscripts**
www.thesoulscripts.com

week 1: build a house

Ephesians 4:12
1 Corinthians 3:10
1 Thessalonians 5:11

I ran into my room, slammed the door, and collapsed on my bed.

I began to cry. Ugly, black mascara rivers flowed down my cheeks and stained my pillow.

Worst day EVER!

My heart was still broken after ending things with that guy, I was grieving the loss of a loved one, and one of my closest friends at the time sent me some hurtful text messages after an argument we had – a wicked combination leaving my heart feeling weary, lonely, and fragile.

For the first time in a long time, I reached for the Bible I brought back to school with me that fall semester. It felt like a big heavy mystery in my lap. It was something I wanted to understand and I knew it held a power I wanted to experience, but I didn't have proper understanding of how to harness it.

Unsure of what else to do, I held the Bible with the edge of the pages facing up toward my sobbing eyes and opened to the pages one of my teardrops landed between (by the way, this is not the best way to read the Bible). It happened to be in the book of 1 Chronicles. Another teardrop fell over a passage on the page – 1 Chronicles 22.

I read about how Solomon's preparations to build a temple for the Lord.

This wasn't exactly the comforting little passage I was hoping for but it intrigued me. I decided to look up the word, "temple," and learned that a synonym for temple is "house of God."

What, God? How is this going to help me feel better? Am I supposed to build a house? I don't know how to build a house.

I kept reading, pondering what it could mean.

I called Habitat for Humanity – a local non-profit that builds homes for the underprivileged in the community. I asked if they had any upcoming builds and explained that it would somehow fix my broken heart.

The woman on the line apologized as she told me she wasn't sure what I meant and apologized again as she explained that she couldn't help me because they didn't have any upcoming builds in the winter.

Okay, God. You got me. I'm stumped. I don't know what you want me to do.

I spent months trying to figure it out with no luck.

A few months later I joined a sorority – something I swore I would never do. Funny how God tends to lead us to places we don't plan on going ourselves, huh?

After spending some time in the sorority, I really started listening for God's voice. I realized that I had spent so much time trying *understand* His will that I failed to really *live* His will.

Then, I had an AH-HA moment. On that cold, sad day when I sobbed onto the pages of my Bible months earlier, God wasn't telling me to build a physical house. He had already provided the physical house, full of His daughters. In that moment He revealed to me my purpose: to build a home for Him in my heart and then to build UP – to build up and encourage His people in love.

Then it hit me:

God, you built me to build!

He built all of us to build. He built us to build up His church, to build up His people, from right where we are and wherever He calls us to – even when that means the places we don't want to go.

I can't say that I completely nailed that challenge during my time in college. I often wonder about all the ways I could have done a better job. However, listening to the stories of my sisters, sharing mine, and openly sharing what God had done in my life gave me more purpose than any of my other endeavors.

God was faithful. By the time I graduated, I had the privilege of developing some of the strongest bonds with women I never would have met had I resisted going where God led me when I didn't understand. I saw two of my best friends experience the tangible presence of God and recommit their lives to the Lord. I saw big changes and major breakthroughs and realized the importance of simply living in God's will instead of trying to understand it.

So, before you think you can't make an impact or leave a legacy for Christ on your campus, remember this one thing:

Stop looking at Jesus as a tool in your tool belt when you are meant to be a tool in His.

If you let Him, He will uniquely use *you* to help build His church. You are a priceless tool in Kingdom building and you have a unique role to play. It simply requires open hands, open ears, and an obedient heart.

Let's get to work.

TALK IT OUT

Have you been treating Jesus more like a tool in YOUR tool belt for accomplishing your blueprints for your life? Or have you been acting like a tool in His tool belt for accomplishing HIS blueprints for His Kingdom?

Identify two gifts, strengths or talents people often say you have or that you know about yourself. (Groups: help each other see your gifts if you get stuck!)

How have you let God put those gifts, strengths, or talents into action in building action? How have you held back?

TRUTH SAYS...

Ephesians 4:11-13 says that God has equipped each of us with gifts for the sake of building up the body of Christ. Our building specializations and skills may look different, but as Christians, we are all equipped and called to build up His church.

1 Corinthians 3:10 is a direct statement of the eternal value of our earthly work. The way we work on earth according to the ways of Christ lives on into eternity. In this passage, Paul is discussing the importance of the work done for community/church building and compares himself to a skilled master builder who has laid the foundation. The foundation that we are built up on is Jesus Christ.

1 Thessalonians 5:10-11 reveals the purpose behind Jesus' death: so that we may live with Him. In doing so, we are to encourage one another and build each other up.

THE BIG IDEA: YOU WERE BUILT TO BUILD

week 2: limitless

Matthew 19:26
Mark 9:23
Ephesians 3:20

My husband and I recently went apple picking and I was having a blast until I realized I couldn't reach the apples near the top of the tree. Most of the good apples on the lower branches had already been picked, and I was growing more and more frustrated by the minute.

There was an abundant supply at the top of the tree but I didn't have any hope of reaching it without help. My husband noticed my frustration and helped me reach the fruit I was longing for. With his help and a little determination, I no longer felt so limited.

The experience reminded me of when I first started writing. Some people advised me not to be too Christian or I would really, "limit myself financially."

I pondered their input.

Could they be right? Should I leave God out of it?

I was tempted to take their advice and strongly considered it for weeks. But deep down I knew couldn't. I didn't want to look like the world. I wanted to trust that God could do more with something small than I could do with something big.

Looking back, I see that what they didn't realize is that we actually limit ourselves by *not* including Jesus in our work. However, we are *limitless with Jesus* in our work. He can do far more with our work and ministry than we could ever dream of doing with all our financial plans, goal sheets, knowledge programs, and more.

The enemy will always try to make us believe that there is not enough to make an eternal impact. He tells us that we have a limited supply of love, grace, people, knowledge, resources, time, and more.

But God tells another story. He promises abundance – more than enough to make an eternal impact. With Him, there is a *limitless* supply of love, grace, people, knowledge, resources, time, and more.

If you're afraid of sharing your faith, reaching outside of your comfort zone, or taking steps toward leaving an eternal legacy right where you are, don't forget that when we are partner with God in His mission, we are **limitless**.

The moment we start letting God boost us up when we feel too small for His mighty mission, the legacy we can leave will reach higher and be more fruitful than we could have ever hoped or dreamed.

He is a God who knows no limits and helps our limited abilities, and He will see to it that our obedience bears much fruit for the Kingdom.

TALK IT OUT

What has discouraged you from doing God's work or reaching out to Him for help in the past?

Do you ever feel limited in leaving a legacy on your campus or in your community? Why?

Have you ever experienced God helping you accomplish something you couldn't have accomplished on your own? How can that situation encourage you in the future?

TRUTH SAYS...

Ephesians 3:20 reminds us that Christ is able to do immeasurably more we could ever ask or imagine when we let Him work through us, so that He alone can get the glory. There is no limit on His glory.

Matthew 19:26 reminds us that all things are possible with God. He speaks and the waves obey Him. He moves and the mountains move. On our own, big things are out of our reach. With God, we are limitless.

Mark 9:23 says that *everything* is possible for one who believes in who Jesus is and in His power (notice this doesn't say, *most* things; it says *everything*).

THE BIG IDEA: YOU ARE LIMITLESS WITH THE LORD

week 3: raising up arrows

Matthew 28:20
John 1:8
John 1:30

I went to Francesca's (my favorite!) to find a dress for an event I had coming up. As soon as I walked into the store, all the cute little knick-knacks they have distracted me from dress shopping. I ended up finding two golden arrows to mount on the wall.

When I got home, I found a hammer and nails and went to work. I hung them on a blank wall and took a step back to admire my work.

As I analyzed how good of a job I did, I realized something.

I am an arrow in God's kingdom. My work, my effort, or my righteousness are not the point. *I am not the point. I'm a pointer to He who is the Point.*

My job in leaving a legacy isn't about being a perfect or pretty display of what a Christian should look like. It's about pointing. It's about loving and helping others become arrows who lead and point others to Jesus as well. The pattern continues, therefore leaving a legacy.

If leaving a legacy were all about our good deeds or examples, we'd be more like a dot. We wouldn't be pointing at anything worth leading others toward and it wouldn't continue. It would stop, right at us, as soon as we leave our particular campus or community. It would simply be a point, and it would be making ourselves the single point instead of pointing.

I'm rambling now, but here's the point (pun intended): Choose to point people to Jesus by the way you love them but don't stop there. Encourage and equip them to do the same. Be present in your community and invest time in raising up arrows, or leaders, to raise up more arrows for the Kingdom long after you leave this place and long after your name has been forgotten.

Raising up arrows is an eternal, outside-of-ourselves kind of impact, because a legacy isn't just a good example – it's something that continues. When it does, it won't matter if our name is remembered or not.

We are not the point. Jesus is the point.

TALK IT OUT

Have you run into any walls when trying to leaving a legacy?
Do you have a hard time building strong connections? Do
you doubt that you are called to leave a legacy? Why?

What steps are you taking to make an eternal difference long
after you leave your community or campus?

Who are some girls that have prayed for and encouraged
you? Who has God put in your life that you could be praying
for and encouraging?

TRUTH SAYS...

Matthew 28:20 is the key part of the Great Commission that
commands us to teach. Teaching is a way to equip. When we
teach or equip others in the ways of Christ, we are raising up
arrows, or disciples. We don't have to do it on our own
because Jesus promises to be with us.

John 1:8 is an example of John's pointing to Jesus that we
ought to mimic. He humbly proclaimed, "I am not the Light
but have come to bear witness to the One who is the Light."
We are not the source of the Light; Jesus is. We are the
shiners of, the witness bearers of, and the pointers to the
source of Light in this dark world.

John 1:30 is another example of humbling ourselves and
exalting Jesus. John knew that even though Jesus was
younger than he was in terms of years on earth, Jesus existed
before he ever did because Jesus is God, who always was and
always will be.

THE BIG IDEA: SIMPLY BEING A GOOD
EXAMPLE MAKES IT ABOUT FURTHURING ME.
LEAVING A LEGACY FOR CHRIST IS ABOUT
FURTHURING THE KINGDOM.

The Struggle is Real:

A Study on Strength Through Sufferings, Setbacks, & Struggles

Hey girlfriend!

I'm so glad you've decided to join this study. You might be going through something hard now, and you might have questions like: *Why would a good God let bad things happen?*

I've asked this question so many times in my journey with the Lord. It's a totally and completely valid question and I think we should talk about because, well, we've all wondered it!

My hope is that this short four-week study will encourage you to see God's purpose and provision through pain, suffering, and disappointments. I pray that it will refresh your heart, remind you that you're not alone, and open your eyes to the good message buried beneath the mud and dirt. Flowers can only grow through dirt, right?

I know the growth is hard and the journey is long, but I believe that sufferings reveal that we are not made for this world but for a better one – a world without pain and suffering. That world exists; it's called God's Kingdom.

Maybe you've not experienced hardship in your own life but have been discouraged by the ugly things you see happening in the world. Or perhaps you've completely hit rock bottom and don't know how to get up.

Whatever kind of hardship you've faced or encountered, let's wrestle with it together and help each other up.

We've all got our struggles, but we don't have to grow through them alone. So, put your gloves on and dig into the dirt with me. Let's uncover the truth beneath the surface, cultivate meaningful conversation, and water the flowers that He has planted deep within the soil of our hearts with Truth. Together with God, we can grow taller and stronger as we uncover the purpose each grain of dirt holds in our life.

Xox,

jordan lee

For more, follow me online!
Facebook: **Jordan Lee**
Instagram: **@soulscripts**
www.thesoulscripts.com

week 1: stinky stuff

John 9:1-12
Luke 18:22-25
Romans 5:2-5
Romans 8:18

My husband recently made dinner for the two of us. The chicken was delicious. The potatoes? To die for. But the brussel sprouts? *NO THANKS!*

Have you ever smelled brussel sprouts? They stink, and they're not that pretty to look at. I could hardly stand that they were touching the chicken on my plate.

I picked at my food, but he was starving after a long day so he shoveled the food into his mouth faster than I could say the words "brussel sprouts." It was painful to watch. But his hunger was slowly satisfied and he regained his energy and strength after he took that last bite.

As I held my breath and gulped down one brussel sprout at a time, I realized something profound and I want to share it with you.

Sometimes life put really stinky things on our plate and sometimes it's really hard to see what possible benefit something so ugly and smelly could possibly have in our life. But the healthiest things for us often aren't the tastiest, right? Sometimes they downright stink. A cupcake would have been easier to eat, but it wouldn't help me grow in any good way (other than my body fat percentage). That's why it's called *junk* food.

When things are easy, they don't grow us or challenge us. Naturally, we begin to believe that we don't have to depend on anyone else but ourselves.

But the sweet thing about stinky stuff – about sufferings, setbacks, and struggles – is that although they may smell absolutely horrible and unappetizing, they are often the very thing we need to grow outside of our comfort zone and strengthen our faith. When we shovel our way through them, when we come out on the other side, and when we conquer that last bite, there's a renewed sense of strength and growth, right?

So, when life hands you something really stinky, remember that growth will "sprout" from it. If you press on, if you trust that Jesus is working through the stinky, messy stuff, it will always be for your greater good and the glory of God. When God is all you have, you'll realize that He is all you need. And that? That's the sweet smell of victory.

TALK IT OUT

What struggle or suffering has been placed in front of you?

How have you handled it? Have you shoveled your way right through it, trusting God every step of the way? Or if you're more like me, are you pushing it as far away from you as possible and plugging your nose? Be honest!

TRUTH SAYS…

John 9:1-12 is the story of Jesus healing a blind man. He could have simply said the word and the man would have been healed; Jesus didn't have to use anything besides His power (compare this healing to the healing in Luke 18:22-25 when Jesus simply said the words). But this time, He reached down into the dirt, made mud with his spit, and smothered it on the man's face. Why do you think he did this? It could have been for a number of reasons; His ways are not our ways. However, it does show us that sometimes we have to trust that in order to experience growth or healing in our faith, we might have to go through some hard and yucky stuff.

Romans 5:2-5 reminds us that the stinky stuff in life (suffering) produces endurance, which produces character. Character produces hope and God's love is poured into us. Only through our trials can our faith grow to new strength. Only through hard stuff can we learn how to endure, grow in our character, and hold onto the hope He offers us. Current sufferings are for our greater good and we will come out on the other side of the trial restored, refreshed, and renewed.

Romans 8:18 tells us that although the current sufferings on our plate may be really stinky, the glory that will result from them is so great that it's not even worthy of comparison. In other words, the goodness that will result will make the present sufferings we are working through seem so small and insignificant that they are not even worth worrying about.

THE BIG IDEA: SUFFERINGS BRING SANCTIFICATION

Sanctity (verb): to make holy or to grow in holiness

week 2: crash landings

Joshua 1:9
Isaiah 41:10

I don't know about you, but I love movies. Movies tell a story. I especially love happy endings. You know, where the hero swoops in and saves the day, the good guy wins, music plays, and fireworks sparkle before the credits roll. Those are the ones that sprinkle a little magic dust over my heart and revive my hope.

I think we all want a happy ending. I think we all want a hero to save us from the struggle and fly us right into the happy ending. But the hard parts, the messy moments, and the crash landings are necessary parts of the story – they are what make happy endings possible.

If you've seen *Superman: The Movie* (1978), you are familiar with the scene where Superman saves Lois Lane from the helicopter. If you haven't, here's the spark notes version: Lois Lane is flying in a helicopter. Said helicopter crashes. Lois dangles high above the ground, holding on for dear life. She holds on for an impressive amount of time. But after a while, she lost strength. As she falls toward her death, when it seems as though all hope is lost, Superman flies in from what seems like out of nowhere. He catches her and says, "Excuse me, Miss, I've got you."

Phew! That was a close one!

Everyone cheers and celebrates the good guy's victory as magic is sprinkled over our hearts. All is right in the world again.

But Lois didn't make that possible. Superman did.

Isn't that something? The hero was nearby all along and he came to the rescue just in the nick of time. However, there would have been no need for a hero and no appreciation of a happy ending if there were no trial.

I liken our lives to a movie. It's a wild adventure, a beautiful work of art, a masterpiece that keeps you on the edge of your seat if you really pay attention. But every now and then there's a scene that's hard to live through. We can't fast forward through the hard parts and we have no way of knowing what will happen as the story evolves. We can only hold on tight as the scene unfolds. But sometimes, as we hold on tight, we begin to believe that we are walking through trials alone and that we have to be strong enough, brave enough, and put together enough in order to survive.

If you're anything like me, you've probably had a handful of crash landings in your life, too. Maybe you've experienced failure or loss or disease, or perhaps you've just been walking through disappointment. When I grieved the loss of a loved one, I felt a lot like Lois Lane. The day my mom had called me to tell me that Nana was taking her final breaths, the helicopter of my life seemed to take a nosedive.

Nana was my best friend and my hero as I grew up. She loved me with a magical, be-anything-you-want, unconditional love. She would dance around the living room to celebrate anything I did – from potty training, to an A on a test, to my first job at the local sandwich shop.

She would celebrate me just for being me. These qualities about her always invited my fragile heart to remember how loved and adored I was, even through the awkward years of crooked teeth and questionable hairstyles.

But the night that I drove alone in the dark to hug her one last time felt totally and completely surreal. The thought of losing her made me shudder. As I relived memories, I could almost feel her strong hug, see her soft smile, and smell her faint scent – a mix of Aveda Shampoo and her famous Spanish rice that she made every time I visited.

I pressed the gas pedal down a bit harder. After what seemed like forever, I finally pulled into town. I swerved into the nursing home parking lot and busted through the front doors. I ran down the wide, long hallways. They were so empty, so cold, and so lonely.

Finally, I collapsed at Nana's bedside. She struggled to breathe. I sobbed as I watched my best friend, the light of my life, in her darkest, weakest hour. I had never experienced such grief. This was something I couldn't hold onto or control. This was real life. This was loss. This was death. And I *hated* it.

Within a few hours her slow breathing came to a halt as her soul floated away. It was over. She was gone.

I collapsed on the bathroom floor and shut the door behind me. I sat on the cold tile, hugged myself, and nearly hyperventilated as I cried ugly tears. I had never felt so small and alone in the world. I wanted to run outside, scream, and send SOS signals into the grey, bleak night sky.

SOS! Crash landing! Send help!

Maybe you've experienced of one of life's crash landings, and perhaps you're holding on for dear life or feeling as if you're dangling alone and losing hope. Maybe you're asking questions like, *Why would God do this to me? Why would He let suffering happen? Why would He break my heart? Am I going to make it through this?*

Sometimes we have to go through some really hard things and maybe even survive a crash to get to the happy ending. If life were perfect, there'd be no need for a happy ending. I can't help but think about how much God is like Superman in our tragedy. He's never early, never late, and always closer than we think.

Jesus' work on the cross guarantees us a happy ending. No matter what happens along the way, regardless of how difficult a certain scene or chapter may be, the story still ends the same: we are guaranteed eternal life with Christ. He says in His Word that we WILL have trial in this life but to have courage, to take heart, because He has overcome the world (John 16:33). So, maybe those are necessary parts of the story that make the happy ending that much sweeter.

The question for us, then, is whether or not we trust in His power to save us. The problem for us in our *do-it-yourself* culture is that we are tempted to trust in our own power and strength instead of God's. It only makes sense to trust His plan though. I mean, He wrote the whole plotline and He never writes a bad story. Maybe there's a bad season, but never a bad ending. God allows us to walk through hard seasons so that we learn to depend on Him – so that He alone can get the glory. We're invited to trust Him in the process, through each and every scene, and to let Him pull it all together as He executes the happy ending according to plan.

Whether you've been trusting God all along, doubting His goodness, or struggling to believe He exists, His invitation for you, too, sister friend.

So, you can let go and stop depending on your own strength. He's got you, sister. He loves you, He is with you, and He's swooping in to carry you to safety. That's a promise that might reignite a little hope in your heart and sprinkle a little magic over your spirit tonight.

TALK IT OUT

Have you ever faced tragedy, or know someone who has? What was this experience like? If you're in a group setting, describe that experience; share what you feel comfortable sharing. If you're doing this study individually, write down your experience in your journal.

How did you see God move through this experience?

TRUTH SAYS...

Joshua 1:9 is a promise from God that He is with us in our trouble, He is with us in our trials and trouble, in the dark places, and in the dry seasons. You aren't alone in your pain, heartbreak, mess, or struggle.

Isaiah 41:10 reminds us not to be afraid, even when it seems as though we are just moments away from our death. God is not far away and He will swoop in and uphold us with His right hand, just like Superman did for Lois Lane but better.

THE BIG IDEA: HARDSHIPS REVEAL OUR NEED FOR THE KIND OF HAPPY ENDING ONLY GOD CAN GIVE

week 3: Comforter vs. comfort

John 14:16
John 16:33
Romans 8:26

It was a cold, rainy night in October. I had just failed an exam in my night class, missed the bus, and found myself shivering as I walked home.

The dreariness of the day and feelings of failure were enough to put me in a bad mood. On top of that, my ex-boyfriend had just posted a picture on Facebook with a new girl, reminding me of all the ways that relationship failed *and* it also happened to be the one-year anniversary of Nana's death.

I felt as if darkness not only surrounded my body but also my tiny, barely-beating heart. I relived that day as I watched her in her final breaths. Jealousy bubbled up inside of me thinking of my ex's new girl. My self-esteem plummeted as I realized I might have to retake statistics class after that test.

Questions raced through my mind as tears filled my eyes:

I still can't believe she's gone.
How did I manage to study all of the wrong material?
Ugh, it's so cold.
Seriously, dude? Do you really need to post that?
Would anyone on this campus come to my rescue right now?
*Would anyone here take a bullet for me? Do I have **real** friends?*
Why is this happening? What are you doing, God?

I felt friendless, hopeless, and to be honest, pretty heartless.

When I finally made it home, the first thing I did was jump in the hot shower, and then I crawled into bed. I pulled my comforter over myself in an attempt to feel just a little bit of comfort after such a depressing evening.

My body warmed up and I fell into a deep sleep.

Maybe you're going through a hard time or struggling with loss, failure, disappointment, heartbreak, or something else. Maybe you feel like you're walking alone through the cold air on a dark and rainy night. Perhaps a tragedy has struck you or someone close to you and you're hurting all over.

Now think about what I looked for the moment I got home on that cold, rainy night. I looked for comfort to ease my pain. I looked for a place to warm up and lay my head, right?

That's great for my physical comfort, but my heart still hurt. What I didn't realize in that moment is that when we walk through hard times, we don't just need a fluffy down comforter – we need **the Comforter**.

If we go to God for comfort, He doesn't just hand us luxurious heart pillows on a silver platter after a long day. What does He do? He gives us His Holy Spirit who is the Comforter. He works from the inside out. He plants His Spirit within us and He comes to live inside the heart that the world has hardened. In doing so, He puts the very comfort of Jesus inside of us as we walk with Him through our pain.

We might have to walk through the cold, frigid air. We might have to be pelted by raindrops and heartache sometimes. In fact, I know we will have to. Jesus told us we would face tragedy and hardship. But we have access to the ultimate Comfort who will walk through that rain with us and shine

His Son upon us to warm our hearts when they grow cold and weary.

Open your little shattered heart to the only One who can make it whole again.

TALK IT OUT

What struggles or hardships have you walked through or are you currently walking through? It can be something as simple as an academic disappointment or something as big as loss or tragedy. All struggles are struggles and we ought to talk about them honestly.

Have you looked for worldly comfort, or have you invited God's Spirit to comfort your heart from the inside out?

Groups: Pray over the girl to your right – lift her current struggle, frustration, disappointment, etc. to God and ask that His Spirit, the ultimate Comforter, come dwell in her heart.

Individuals: Write down your answers to these questions and your prayer for God's Spirit to comfort you in the midst of these struggles.

TRUTH SAYS...

John 14:16 is Jesus' promise that God will give us the Comforter, His Spirit, to come live within us forever. Not just for a moment or a season, not just when we do our Christian stuff right, but *forever* – whenever we open our hearts to His help.

In John 16:33, Jesus doesn't say that we might have trouble. He says that we *will* have trouble in this life. But, we aren't left without hope. We can take heart, or in other words, have courage and find comfort, in knowing that He has overcome every trouble this world could throw at us.

Romans 8:26 illustrates the role of the Spirit. The Holy Spirit helps us in our weaknesses, intercedes on our behalf, and intersects our pains when we don't have words to say. The Holy Spirit lifts our hearts to God in a way we could not do on our own in the midst of our pain and suffering.

THE BIG IDEA: ETERNAL COMFORTER > EARTHLY COMFORT

week 4: disappointed

Joshua 5-6
Isaiah 55:8-9
John 15:5
Romans 8:28

My husband played four years of Division 1 college football. Since then, he has countless hours training and working to achieve his goal of making it into the next level. However, playing professionally hasn't proved to be as easy as we would have liked it to be.

The first year that he went through the NFL draft, several NFL coaches told him he would certainly have many teams interested in signing him. He was ranked in the top five long snappers in his class. He had a great agent working for him. He was bound to get several calls on draft day.

You can imagine our confusion when that expected call didn't come. He was confused. I was confused. His agent was confused. His coaches and teammates were confused. We were all confused.

The silence was deafening.

Eventually, he did get a call and had an opportunity to try out for a team. He performed really well and the coaches were impressed, but despite his stellar performance, the end result didn't go as we wished. For reasons outside of his control, he wasn't signed and he nearly hung up his cleats after that experience.

But with just enough spark to keep going, he trained for a few more months. Seemingly out of nowhere, the same team called him back a few months later and signed him as a free agent right before the next draft.

I remember thinking, *"This is it. We've made it! Finally!"*

Except it *wasn't* it. After eight months, he was released – just two weeks before our wedding day. We were back to square one and more disappointed than ever.

My heart broke for him. He had worked so hard, persevered, and trained through adversity for long enough. *He deserved this.*

As I moped around, feeling sorry for him and wondering what we would do or where we would go after getting married, I was challenged by an excerpt from a booked titled *Radical* by David Platt:

"The dangerous assumption we unknowingly accept in the American dream is that our greatest asset is in our own ability. The American dream prizes what people can accomplish when they believe in themselves and trust in themselves, and we are drawn toward such thinking. But the gospel has different priorities. The gospel beckons us to die to ourselves and to believe in God and trust in His power. In the gospel, God confronts us with our utter inability to accomplish anything apart from him... this, after all is the goal of the American Dream: to make much of ourselves. But the goal of the gospel is to make much of God." [1]

I'm sure you've faced setbacks and disappointment when pursuing a goal or chasing a dream. Maybe they've even knocked you off your feet and stolen your hope. Join the club.

But we have to remember that *every single thing we accomplish in life isn't about our performance but God's purpose.* In order to let us experience His power, He places us in situations where we are desperate for His power so that the only explanation for things working out is none other than His provision.

When we work hard, set goals, and chase our dreams, the challenge becomes: are we making much of God or much of ourselves? Are we believing in our own abilities or God's abilities in and through us?

He works through our disappointments, uncertainties, and let downs so that we learn to depend on His power over our performance. He can do far more and far better things with His power than we could ever dream of doing on our own – even on our best days with our best possible performance.

Stop trying to fix or control whatever setback or let down you've recently experienced. He will work it out by His power, not yours. When you depend on His power, you will experience the abundant fruit of His provision instead of the fruitless efforts of your performance.

TALK IT OUT

What disappointments have you recently faced?

How did you feel toward God in the middle of that disappointment? Resentful? Grateful? Dependent? Something else?

Have you been relying on God's power or on your own performance?

TRUTH SAYS...

Joshua 5-6 is a story of God's power on display. If you read Joshua 6:3-5, you will see that God's plan for His people to defeat the walls of Jericho was set up so that in the end, only He could get the glory. He didn't ask Joshua's army to storm the castle walls or fight to win. He asked them to obey what seemed like a foolish command: *march around the walls of Jericho for seven days, and on the seventh day, march seven times and blow your trumpets then give a loud shout.* When they obeyed, the walls came tumbling down. David Platt teaches that the only explanation was God's power at work – the army's effort wasn't what brought down the walls, their obedience was.[2]

Isaiah 55:8-9 are the words of God, declaring the truth about His ways. He is a miracle worker; His power trumps our efforts every single time. He can move mountains, heal, save redeem, forgive, destroy, and do all things. He can do all things beyond our understanding, and sometimes it takes a painful disappointment to teach us this reality and strengthen our faith and trust. We can't always know His ways or thoughts, but we can always trust His promises.

John 15:5 is God's confrontation of our inability to accomplish anything apart from Him. Every success we have and every work we do is a result of Him at work in our life. However, when we are so busy working hard, we tend to forget that we couldn't possibly work hard without His provision in sustaining our very life.

Romans 8:28 reminds us that we have to be more reliant on God working things out for our good than working out our own good. He calls us according to His purpose and establishes our steps each step of the way.

THE BIG IDEA: HIS PURPOSE & POWER > MY PURPOSE & PERFORMANCE

week 5: is God listening?

Psalm 34:17
John 11

When my best friend was dying several years ago, I cried out to God. I asked Him to heal her. I begged Him to change the circumstances. Within twenty-four hours of saying that prayer, she passed away.

I remember asking, "God, are you even listening to me?"

Last year, I spent months working on a book proposal. When it was finally finished, I sent it to my agent and we submitted it to several publishers. The weeks we waited for responses felt like years.

Over the course of those 6-8 weeks, I spent a lot of time in prayer. I prayed that God would give me the right publishing partner, that he would bless me with a book deal that would bring Him glory.

And then? No book deal. Not one. Nada. Zip. Zilch. Zero. I was crushed.

I didn't understand. Why was God ignoring my prayer again?

Maybe you've experienced much worse circumstances than the few I just shared, maybe not. But I'd be willing to bet that you've wondered if God is listening to your prayers at all.

If so, I want to whisper to you a truth I was recently both challenged and comforted by:

Just because God doesn't give us the answer we want doesn't mean He's not listening to us. He sees the whole picture when we only see a speck of it.

Sometimes, God uses hardships and disappointments to break us – to break our pride, stubbornness, and selfishness. In doing so, He is preparing us for a greater glory.

I now realize how much I was making prayer about my will and not about God's will. But the entire point of prayer is to help us reflect Jesus more and more – and Jesus surrendered. Tim Keller puts it this way, "The basic purpose of prayer is not to bend God's will to mine, but to mold my will into His."[2]

If I had gotten what I wanted handed to me on a silver platter, or if God would have answered me in the way I wanted at the time, I never would have gotten to know God or experienced the sweetness of His drawing me near to Himself in the middle of life's trouble.

Although I don't know whether or not answering you the way that you'd like right now, I do know that He *is* listening. With Jesus, it's never over, even after death.

Since He is the God of the universe who sees all that we cannot see, we can trust His all-knowing wisdom over our tiny glimpse of understanding.

TALK IT OUT

Have you ever felt like God isn't listening to your prayers
when He doesn't answer you how you want? How do you
respond or react when you feel as though your prayers are
not being heard?

When circumstances are challenging, have you been tempted
to give up on prayer altogether? What has helped you
continue praying, even when it's hard?

TRUTH SAYS...

Psalm 34:17 says that God hears our cries. Our prayers never
go unheard. They may just not be answered how we *think*
they ought to be because God knows how they *need* to be
answered.

John 11 is a passage that shows us the importance of God's
answer over the answer we want. In this passage, Lazarus is
sick, about to die. His sisters, Martha and Mary, send word to
Jesus in hopes that He will come quickly and heal Lazarus.
But Jesus doesn't; He waits. After Lazarus dies, Jesus goes to
see the sisters. Martha sees Jesus and says, "If you would
have been here, if you would have answered sooner, this
wouldn't have happened!"

Joanna Weaver teaches that if He would have answered her
the way she wanted, He could not have taught her the
foundational truth of the gospel ("I am the resurrection") and
given her the chance to respond.[3] Then, He displayed the
power of God by raising Lazarus to life four days after he
died. This was His answer – and it was even more important
than healing her brother because it radically changed her

faith and understanding of Jesus.[4] The most important thing is that we know Jesus, and sometimes we have to be broken down so that we can know Him.

THE BIG IDEA: PRAYER IS DESIGNED TO CHANGE MY HEART.

Let's Connect!

Defeating the Distraction, Comparison, and Competition of Social Media

Hey girlfriend!

Thanks so much for "following" this study!

I know our hearts and minds are blasted with information constantly. We live in a world that speaks the language of social media, and I know it can be really loud and distracting, which makes it hard to even experience or understand God.

Maybe you're a social butterfly, always tweeting and sharing your latest happenings or thoughts. Or perhaps you're more introverted, entertained by everyone else's social life blasted on the Internet. Maybe you have a bad case of FOMO (Fear Of Missing Out) every time you see what everyone else is up to. Or maybe, just maybe, you've done what I once did and deleted all your accounts to avoid the frustration social media can cause.

Regardless of your current social media status, my hope for this study is that we break down the realities of social media one piece at a time. In doing so, we'll defeat the damaging lies that social media tells us about ourselves.

The world of social media all too often turns into a place of comparison. Just the other day I made a wonderful dinner for my husband and I, spending a whole fifteen minutes microwaving the meal. I put it on our boring plates and felt pretty good about myself.

I CREATED FOOD YOU CAN EAT, WHAT?! GO, ME!

Ten minutes after setting the table, I happened to open Instagram only to see a photo someone *else* posted of an exquisitely garnished meal on their perfect little table in their perfect little house. It made me feel small. It made me resent the 30-year-old hand me down table and simple microwave meal I just made. I lost appreciation for the gift of food and fellowship because I was comparing my insides to someone else's outsides.

Maybe you've done that too. Maybe you've also lost sight of the gifts God has given you when scrolling through your news feed. But I think if we learned to see God in the midst of it, we might have a renewed and refreshed heart.

So log into this one with me. Upload your profile picture, let's be friends – with each other and with the King of the Social Network... I mean, the Universe.

Xox,

jordan lee

For more, follow me online!
Facebook: **Jordan Lee**
Instagram: **@soulscripts**
www.thesoulscripts.com

week 1: like

Genesis 1:27
Zephaniah 3:17
John 3:16
Romans 12:6

A recent study done by psychologists at the University of Albany found that the experience of watching a social media post rocket in popularity stimulates the same area of the brain that smoking crack cocaine does.[1]

It may seem like a dramatic metaphor, but study after study has shown how the desire for social media is a really a deep desire for validation. We crave likes because we crave love. Likes are a tangible currency by which we can measure our worth, value, and overall validity.

And we DO. But just because we *can* doesn't mean we *have* to.

We *can* turn to social media in search of likes, or we can turn to God in search of love.

I know what you're thinking:
So cliché.
Easier said than done.
Okay, but I still like when my picture gets likes.

Yes, I know. I still like when my pictures get likes, too. My work is something I search for validation in as well. I'm right there with you.

We're all searching for validation; everything humans do is in search of validation. The truth is that we're just searching in the wrong places 99% of the time, even when deep down we know the best validation comes from God.

So, it's not about whether or not we are searching for it, but *where* we are searching for it.

Maybe you're searching for likes from cyberspace. Or perhaps in your peer group, organization, professional accomplishments, Greek house, social club, the classroom, or maybe even your Christian group. #wut? It's a real thing. We search for it everywhere.

Wherever you're looking for likes, let me remind you that you're really searching for a love only God can give. No number of likes will ever be enough for any sustainable amount of time.

Can you just do me a favor and log off the mentality that says your validation comes from what you can produce, how clever your captions are, and how involved you are in every single thing on campus? Great.

Because it doesn't – and it's time to take your life back.
#nottodaysatan
#sorrynotsorry
#blessed

TALK IT OUT

What lie do you fight the most when it comes to your validation or worth?

Where do you search for validation most? Social media? Friends? Peers? Academics?

TRUTH SAYS...

Genesis 1:27 and Zephaniah 3:17 tell us that God made us in HIS image and delights in us, just as we are.

John 3:16 is a profound reminder of His love for us even when we are unlovable. Even when our lives don't look likable, even when we don't have the greatest presentations or cutest of captions, He loves us. He loves us when we are unfiltered and unlovable – to the point of death. A thumbs up on Facebook could never do that.

Romans 12:6 reminds us that he has given us validation by instilling in us gifts, talents, and strengths.

THE BIG IDEA: LIFE > LIKES

week 2: follow

Matthew 16:24
John 8:12
1 Peter 2:21

The other day I saw a cute little duck family cross the street.
A-DOR-A-BLE.

Seven little ducklings followed Mama Duck around, trusting
her guidance completely. They followed her into dangerous
places without hesitating. If mom was going to cross a busy
street, you'd better believe little ducklings were going to be
right there with her. They trusted she'd lead them safely to a
bigger and better pond.

As I watched a little bit of nature's sweetness unfold, I was
reminded of the reality of following. Following is so much
deeper than what we've turned it into in the world of social
media.

I think a more appropriate term for following someone on
social media is "stalking" or perhaps even "admiring."

Because what is it, really? It's looking into their life.
Checking out what they're doing. Perhaps even ogling over
them or envying their every move. Maybe because it's
interesting, but regardless of the reason, following someone
on social media really isn't following at all, at least not the
way Jesus intended it to be for our hearts.

When He calls us to follow Him, He isn't interested in our
admiration. He is interested in our abandonment – our
abandonment of trust in all earthly things. He never intended

to keep us at an arms distance, allowing us to simply watch from afar and peer into His inspirational life. He invited us in. He cleared the way to a better place.

When we follow Him, really follow Him, we allow ourselves to leave our comfort zone, step into the unknown and into dangerous journeys, trusting all along in His protection and purpose, just like the little ducklings.

The next time you begin to worry about how many followers you have, or when you begin to envy someone you "follow" online, ask yourself:

*Am I looking **up or out**?*

We're all following something, but perhaps we need to fix our focus on Who goes before us – not on who surrounds us. Look up, not out. Keep following, my fellow little ducky, keep following.

TALK IT OUT

Have you ever felt jealous of someone you follow online?

What else have you followed besides Jesus? In other words, what else or who else do you trust with your security and life, perhaps without realizing it? Maybe your job? Your friends? Your grades? Money? Something else?

TRUTH SAYS...

Matthew 16:24 says that following Jesus requires denial of our own comfort. It's comfortable to stay on the safe side, to watch from afar and maybe even admire. But Jesus challenges to go all in, head first, and take the plunge in the deepest waters with Him.

John 8:12 is the words of Jesus. He reminds us that following Him is a path full of light and void of darkness.

1 Peter 2:21 reminds us that Jesus is deserving of our following. He gave up everything for us. True following challenges us to do the same.

THE BIG IDEA: LOOK UP, NOT OUT

week 3: comment

2 Timothy 3:16
Romans 10:17
Revelation 3:20

Sometimes I'm really awkward. Sometimes I say things and then I'm like, "Wow, why'd I just say that?!"

Ever been there? If not, lucky you.

But if you're like most of us, you've probably worried about saying or doing the wrong thing at some point in your life.

I got to thinking about commenting on social media because it's a revolutionary form of communication that allows us to hide behind a screen and voice our thoughts, encouragement, criticism, opinions, and more.

Maybe you've been on the receiving end of some of those comments. Maybe you've been both praised and cut down, either on social media or in real life. Perhaps you've commented the typical, "LOVE THIS!"

Or maybe you've rolled your eyes at comment threads full of arguments, hate, strong opinions, and very little grace.

The world is loud. The internet very well might be louder. If you've been overwhelmed by the noise, if you're drowning in the comments and afraid of being YOU because of the comments you may receive, let's quiet the noise and redirect our communication. Because I think in all of our commenting, connecting, and creating online, we forget to connect and communicate with our Creator.

If the world of social media has been as distracting for you as it can be for me, I invite you to quit commenting in cyberspace for a little while. It's a tiny little kingdom that can't really love you back and it's going to fade away one day. Start *really* connecting – with your Creator and His creation – for the sake of the Kingdom that always was and will always be.

Have a conversation with Him. Pay attention to the little comments He gives you through His creation. Reach out. Make connections (not just on LinkedIn). Love big because you've been loved. He hasn't hesitated to communicate that love to you in His Word. You've just got to create an account – you've got to say yes. Close the apps and open His Word. I promise, you'll find the comments and captions to be much more life giving than those on any social media thread.

TALK IT OUT

Do you enjoy regular communication with God – or do you have a hard time hearing Him in this loud world?

What gets in the way of communicating and connecting with God most?

When do you feel most connected with the Lord and His people?

TRUTH SAYS...

2 Timothy 3:16 reminds us that God's Word is trustworthy for communication, teaching, and growing in goodness.

Romans 10:17 says that faith comes by hearing from the Word of Christ. We cannot produce our own faith. It's a gift that we're given, and we can only experience and take hold of it when we listen and hear His Word in our heart. When the world around us is loud, it's incredibly difficult to experience a living, breathing walk with Jesus in faith.

Revelation 3:20 tells us that Jesus wants to come sit with us. He wants to hang out in our hearts, to have conversation with us, to be a part of our every moment. He's knocking on the door of your heart – have looked up from your phone, let Him in, and sat down for coffee recently?

THE BIG IDEA: COMMUNICATION > COMMENTING

week 4: share

1 Peter 2:9
Matthew 28:18-20
John 13:34

A few months ago, I saw the cutest video ever on Facebook.

THE WORLD NEEDS TO SEE THIS!

I immediately hit the Share button. No hesitation. No second thoughts. I just SHARED it.

I got to thinking how amazing it would be if we shared Jesus with the same boldness and enthusiasm as we do videos on Facebook.

Not sharing Him necessarily in a preachy, obnoxious way but in a real life, outpouring love kind of way. I think we hesitate to share Jesus when we feel as though we don't know enough of the Bible or fear rejection. But if we realized that sharing Jesus STARTS with sharing LOVE, perhaps we wouldn't be so afraid. Maybe we'd hit that button and just SHARE it with the world.

But the hard part about sharing love is that it takes more effort than hitting a button. It requires action and investment. It requires time and energy, right?

We live in a world that says not to give too much away. It says to PUT YOURSELF FIRST. We live in a world that is focused on being served over serving. But are we really gaining when we do that? Are we really gaining anything more than a little bit of luxury that holds no earthly weight?

221

I don't know about you, but I'd rather have a life over luxury – real, world-changing life that holds eternal weight. I'd rather give away love and gain life, true, soul-filling LIFE.

So, don't be afraid to SHARE. Don't be afraid to go outside your comfort zone. Don't be afraid of haters or people who hit the thumbs down button when you do. This life isn't about showing off on social media but sharing love in the brokenness of this world.

And love? Love is Jesus.

Let's make this thing go viral.

TALK IT OUT

What holds you back from sharing the love of Jesus? Doubt? Fear? Feeling like you don't know enough? Something else?

Share with the group (or write down in your journal) a time you experienced someone sharing the love of Jesus with you. How did it change you?

Have you ever had, and taken, the opportunity to share the gospel with someone? How did you see God move in that situation?

TRUTH SAYS...

1 Peter 2:9 says that we are chosen to proclaim His message. When we feel un-choose-able, we are chosen. We are part of something bigger than ourselves, and it's in our job description to share and invite others into the royal priesthood by the way we love.

Matthew 28:18-20 is the Great Commission. Jesus gave us the command to GO, to SHARE, and to LOVE. But He didn't ask us to do anything He hasn't already done, and He doesn't ask us to do it alone. Jesus is always online and available to chat with us. He's with us, regardless of how unqualified we think we are. When we step out in faith, He steps in our place.

John 13:34 is the command to love because Jesus loves us when we least deserve it. Our love should not be motivated by our own self-interest but by the reality that if we have been loved at our worst, we can share it when would rather put our own needs first.

THE BIG IDEA: SHARE LOVE, GAIN LIFE

This Changes Everything:

Conquering the Challenges of Being a Christian in College

Hey girlfriend!

I know, college is hard. Being a Christian in college? Even harder.

It's not a cool thing to do. It's never easy to go against the flow, to challenge the culture, and to stand by something the world wants to write off. The reality is that the gospel is offensive – not because it's bad but because it exposes to the light the pieces of ourselves we would rather hide in the dark.

For a while when I was in college, I had a hard time making God-honoring decisions without coming across to my peers as a prude, boring, or judgmental. I wanted people to like what I did and I wanted God to like what I did. I was afraid to be "too Christian" because I honestly believed that my life would be boring if I was. I felt overwhelmed because in the classroom, I was told truth is relative. At frat parties, I was told Truth is irrelevant. But in my heart, I craved Truth. I just didn't know how to live accordingly.

Perhaps you've felt that struggle. Maybe you're having a hard time really living out your faith – or perhaps even holding onto it. Before we hop into this study, I hope you know that it's okay to wrestle, to ask questions, to struggle, and even to doubt. Just don't keep those feelings bottled up, because when you do they very well might consume you.

Over these next few weeks, I'm going to be really honest with you. I hope you'll find it in your heart to be real, raw, open, and honest with this, too.

College is hard but Jesus is better, and with a little soul searching, Truth talking, and honest conversation, we're going to experience that reality together.

Cool? Okay, cool.

Xox,

jordan lee

For more, follow me online!
Facebook: **Jordan Lee**
Instagram: **@soulscripts**
www.thesoulscripts.com

week 1: a new pair of jeans

2 Corinthians 5:17
Ephesians 4:22-24
Romans 6:4

I recently bought a new pair of jeans and was reminded of a sermon my pastor shared on Ephesians 4:20-24. In this sermon, he compared new life in Christ to getting a new pair of jeans.[1] New jeans can be an exciting purchase, but they can also be incredibly uncomfortable. They aren't broken in and they don't quite mold to us like the old, broken in ones did.

I was excited to wear the new jeans after buying them, but then I noticed myself doing exactly what my pastor had talked about in that sermon so many years back. I didn't throw out the old jeans. I kept them. Every now and then, I'd reach for the old jeans – the comfy ones.

My pastor compared that tendency to how we sometimes treat new life in Christ—sometimes we reach back for our old, comfortable ways, even when God has given us new life[2].

Personally, when I first began a relationship with Jesus, when I first stepped into new life, I was excited! But I noticed that it wasn't comfortable. It challenged me to sacrifice, to serve, and to be transformed and taken outside of my comfort zones.

My pastor taught that we tend to wish that the new life would *mold to me*, rather than allowing myself to be molded to Jesus. He shared that when we choose new life with Jesus, it

228

will feel uncomfortable at first. It's very easy to reach in the back of the drawer and wear what's comfortable. But that we were designed for the new life of God, not for the way we tend to be comfortable living.[3]

New life will challenge us to step outside of our comfort zone, but we were created to be transformed by Christ and to do His work.

I know that in college, it's really hard not to settle for the old, comfortable way. It's incredibly uncomfortable to step into the life God has called us to, because the idea of taking off the old and putting on the new goes beyond taking off misbehavior and putting on righteousness.

But it's so much more than a simple behavior change – it's a heart change, an inside-out change. It's for the ultimate purpose of living in the world as Jesus would – partnering with God in furthering His kingdom right on your campus. It's the greatest and most rewarding assignment one can be given – and because of His power, you have the power to do it.

But first, you've got to step into His love and change more than your outfit. You've got to let Him change your heart.

TALK IT OUT

Do you notice yourself falling into old habits even if you've already become a Christian?

Are you still wearing old pants? Have you gotten comfortable with a lukewarm, passive faith?

If you haven't stepped into new life with Jesus, what is causing you hesitation?

What is the most uncomfortable or challenging part of living life God's way in college for you?

TRUTH SAYS...

2 Corinthians 5:15-17 is a powerful reminder of the exchange that is made when we surrender our lives to the only One who can save us. We are completely reliant Him for our salvation because we cannot earn our own salvation. It's a life we have to step into fully and completely, with no strings attached.

Ephesians 4:22-24 urges us to take off our old self, which belongs to a life before knowing Jesus, and instead put on the new self that reflects the image and likeness of God in true righteousness and holiness. This doesn't mean to manage your external behavior to look like a church girl; it means surrendering your broken pieces to the only One who can make you both whole and holy. Holy means "perfect," and perfection isn't something we can create by our own behavior. It's something only Jesus can give us.

Romans 6:4 tells us that Jesus took on the wrath of God that we deserved and conquered sin and death through His resurrection so that we might walk in the newness of life. When the new life is uncomfortable, challenging, and uncool on campus, remember how much more discomfort and pain Jesus went through for your sake – for the sake of your new life. Let *that* motivate you toss out the old jeans for good.

THE BIG IDEA: TOSS OUT THE OLD, ROTTEN, LIFE FULL OF HOLES AND STEP INTO THE NEW, REDEEMED LIFE FULL OF HIS HOLINESS AND WHOLENESS

week 2: knowing God personally

John 1:1-18
1 Peter 1:20-21
Romans 1:20

Let's talk about Beyoncé because, well, who doesn't want to talk about Beyoncé?

If I had never heard of her, I could find out what she is with a simple Google search. I'd learn that she is a singer, songwriter, record producer, and actress. I know that she is 5'7", was raised in Houston, TX, and that her net worth is $450 million as of June 2016. *Casual...*

I know a lot *about* Beyoncé but I (unfortunately) do not *know* Beyoncé.

What's the difference?

Well, I've never had a conversation with her. I don't know *who* she is at her core. I don't know her heart, her plans, her personal story, or her true identity. I don't share a relationship with her. I just know about her through what the media has told me. I don't love her on a personal level. If she died, it would be a bummer and I might even feel sad, but I most likely wouldn't be sent into physical or emotional grieving, because my heart is not attached to or dependent on hers.

Similarly, it's very common for us to know *about* God based on what we read online, what we heard in church growing up, and even what we see on social media. We can hear what He is – the Creator and Sustainer of the universe, the Author and Perfecter of faith, etc. But that doesn't mean we *know who* God is.

My senior year of college, I did all sorts of Christian-y things. I even led my sorority Bible study and served on leadership for a campus ministry. But then I was challenged by the following question:

If I'm not pained to the core by the thought of His death on the cross, if I haven't built a personal relationship through shared discussion and dialogue, and if I haven't really gotten to know His heart through His Word, *then do I really know Him at all?*

When we don't know someone, it's incredibly difficult to really make that person a priority in our day to day lives. Growing in a relationship requires noticing and paying attention to the other. If I never turned off my devices, clocked out of work, and spent time with my husband, our marriage would crumble faster than a soggy cookie in a cup of milk. If I never took time out of my week to not only meet a friend for coffee but also to *listen* to what she shares about her life, her heart, her faith, dreams, and more, well you can bet that that relationship would suffer and that friend and I would inevitably grow apart.

The same goes for God. He's a wild, adventurous, passionate God in pursuit of your heart. Notice. Pay attention. Make dating a priority with Him. Don't put Him in a box because you've been raised to think a relationship with God is a boring, religious requirement. It's an adventure! It's like dating and adventuring with your best friend, without boundaries or borders.

Open your heart, girlfriend. Don't be afraid to get to know the God of both love and wrath, the God who is at once powerful and present in your tiny corner of the universe. Let His Word be your guide and dive into the adventure. It's not a homework assignment or a matter of checking boxes. Unlike Beyoncé, God is always accessible, available, and ready to show you *who* He is.

Before we know it, the whole "following Jesus" thing won't feel so much like a chore – not even in college.

TALK IT OUT

Do you feel like your relationship with God looks more like your relationship with Beyoncé or with a close friend?

What about college makes it challenging for you to dive into a deeper relationship with God?

Do you hesitate to live out your faith boldly? If so, why? Fear? Stress? Uncertainty? Something else?

TRUTH SAYS...

John 1:1-18 says that God revealed Himself most clearly in Jesus, who is the Word of God made flesh. In other words, God is revealed and experienced when we study His Word. His presence is with us when we make studying Scripture a priority (which beats studying for a math test and holds a lot more eternal weight in our lives). It makes our relationship with God more tangible and applicable when the world discourages us from holding onto it.

1 Peter 1:20-21 says that to have the Word of God is to have God Himself, because when Scripture speaks, God speaks. God has given us a direct tool for hearing Him and communicating with Him. Just because it's not an iPhone or tablet doesn't mean it doesn't work. Every day we have an invitation to personally encounter Him, learn from Him, and grow with Him.

Romans 1:20 reminds us that we not only have access to God through His Word but also through His world. If we pause and take time to look, we will see His power and divinity revealed. We can dip our toes in the waves and get to know

His power. We can breathe in the crisp autumn air and get to know His peace. We can hug a sister and get to know His love and feel His embrace. You see, we have to get to know God. He is in every good thing, everywhere, all the time. We just have to pay attention. When we do, we will hear Him, see Him, and feel Him.

THE BIG IDEA: YOU HAVE 24/7, PERSONAL ACCESS TO THE GOD OF THE UNIVERSE. IT'S TIME TO TAP INTO IT.

week 3: playing the part

2 Corinthians 12:9
James 5:16

In middle school, I began to explore my creative side. I told my mom I was interested in theatre and that I wanted to take acting classes.

However, I didn't want the girls on the soccer team to know. I didn't want them to think that I wasn't interested in soccer anymore. I wanted them to view me as a dedicated teammate, tough to the core. What I didn't realize at the time was that every time I put that jersey and those cleats on, I was acting. I was being what I thought the world around me wanted me to be – an athlete, a winner, a goal scorer.

Anyway, Mom and I kept my blossoming acting career a secret between us.

Once a week, I would hop in Mom's car after school and she would drive me downtown to a tiny little building on the corner where nine or ten other kids gathered. At the beginning of class, we were each assigned a role.

At first, I was painfully shy on stage. I was afraid to say or do the wrong thing. I was afraid that I wouldn't be funny or interesting enough. I spoke my lines with hesitation and shaky knees.

The teacher often told me I needed to be more convincing, so I tried harder. Slowly but surely, I got used to it. Over weeks of training, I became a better and better actress. I learned tips and tactics for acting out different personalities, taking on different character traits, and expressing emotions I wasn't actually feeling.

When show time rolled around, I nailed it. I completely nailed it. I took on the character I wanted the crowd to see, I said my lines with emotions I wasn't actually feeling, and nearly convinced myself that I *was* the character on the stage.

I bowed and hustled off the stage as the crowd broke out in applause.

Looking back on that experience and the decade that followed it, I realized how much the tools and tactics for taking on a certain character trickled into my personal life.

I loved the applause, the reward of a job well done. So, I did a lot of acting – often without even realizing it. I took on the character I thought the world wanted me to be. When I left for college, I took on the character of the fun, social butterfly at frat parties and in the classroom, I took on the character of the serious, dedicated student. I could go on for pages, but I'm sure you get the point.

Somewhere in the middle of it, I lost who I was. I wasn't even sure who was buried beneath all my layers of acting. I was so obsessed with being a good example that I failed to be an honest example. The problem with acting is that it doesn't leave room for vulnerability.

I should probably add a disclaimer that I'm not condemning acting as a career or hobby. This is simply an example to show how easy it is to put on an act, to paint ourselves in the light we want to be seen in instead of actually stepping into the Light and exposing the parts we'd rather not let the world see.

Vulnerability is about letting our true selves be seen. A person that has been transformed by Jesus is someone who can peel back the curtain of their heart and allow the Light to shine through every crack and expose every weakness in their being. It's at once risky and rewarding. It takes courage to open up and expose our brokenness, but it's what we desperately need for true, honest, world-changing connection with both God and His people.

When we become obsessed with *acting* like a good Christian, we build barriers around our hearts that stop us from *experiencing* the real connection that our souls need with God and others. We can only share God's love with others when we open up enough to expose His healing, working hand in our lives to the world.

The beauty of the gospel is that it gives us the freedom and confidence to do just that – to be vulnerable and courageously create those connections with an unshakeable confidence in Christ.

It's a world changing type of confidence, because it does not rest in ourselves but in the God inside of us. When we really know Jesus, acting is unnecessary because there's no character we can create for ourselves that makes the cut.

You can take the mask off. You can drop the filters. You can be honest with your classmates, you can share your struggles with your sisters, and you can talk about the hard stuff. Our walk with God isn't on a graded on a curve and it isn't something we can learn in a class. Living it out doesn't require us to *act* but instead requires us to take *action* – to love, and to love is to be vulnerable.

People don't need to see you, and they don't need to see me. They need to see *Him* at work inside of you and me.

So, peel back the curtain, step aside, and give Him center stage.

TALK IT OUT

Have you ever felt like you're putting on an act or just going through the motions to maintain your Christian status? Have you ever been put off by Christians who try to maintain an image of perfection?

Do you ever feel like you can't talk about the mistakes you've made, the struggles you face, or the weaknesses you walk with? Are you afraid of being vulnerable, worried that people may misjudge you?

How does your life shine God's light? How are you intentionally pointing to Him right now? In what ways could you improve?

TRUTH SAYS...

2 Corinthians 12:9 highlights the importance of humility and vulnerability. Christ's redeeming power is made perfect in our weakness. If we never let it show, we deny God's power and don't allow it to be made manifest in our life

James 5:16 says to confess your sins to one another so that we may be healed. This a profound truth that shows us that confession is not something we should do out of obligation, but because it gives our souls the very thing we need in our brokenness – healing. Exposing our weakness to the light and getting the burdens off our chest glorifies Jesus, lightens our load spiritually, and therefore heals us from guilt and shame.

THE BIG IDEA: NO ACTING NECESSARY. JUST ACTION.

week 4: thriving over surviving

Matthew 24:14
John 4:14
Romans 12:2

I have a cute little cactus that sits on my windowsill. Once, I gave it far too much water and it almost died. So, I stopped watering it all together and now it looks like a raisin and a porcupine had a baby.

I've never really been trained on how to raise a cactus, so the poor little guy is struggling along, barely surviving (who knew it was so complicated?!). I mean, it's definitely not dead yet, but it's not doing well either. Maybe the constant temperature change or the environment in our house has something to do with it.

Anyway, when I look at that poor little cactus, I'm reminded of the difference between merely surviving and abundantly thriving. To thrive is to grow or develop vigorously, to prosper and flourish. But to survive is to exist in spite of hardship, to remain alive, pull through, and simply hold on.

When I think of my soul like that little cactus, I realized how many times in college I settled for merely surviving: surviving through long weeks, somehow managing to put pants on each morning and say a quick prayer before bed.

Maybe that sounds like you. Maybe you're having a really hard time following Jesus in the craziness of college. The easy thing to do, the simple way to fit in, is to follow the crowd. I know because I tried it. I didn't dare to be different because I was afraid my social life, and therefore my happiness and acceptance, would completely die. So, I didn't give my faith much water or Son-light. I was just getting through the days, going through my routine, and doing what the world wanted me to do because I was afraid of being different. My spirit felt like a raisin porcupine – dry, lifeless, and a little bit prickly.

Why?

Because faith is something we cannot live without. There's no fear that a little bit of faith in God can't overcome. If you're afraid of living out your faith in an environment that challenges it daily, remember what fear is.

"Fear is faith misplaced. Fear is *faith* in the wrong thing."
–Joseph Murphy[4]

When it's hard to live our faith, to walk with Jesus, and to press on when we are persecuted, we have to look at what we are placing our faith in – is it in Jesus who promises eternal treasure? Or in ourselves? In others' opinions?

When we place our faith in ourselves and others, we are merely surviving in the harsh environment around us. The reality is that when we do that, we're barely filled with enough water and Son-light to make it through.

Living in a college environment can bring discouragement and doubt to our faith. It may even come with growing pains and dry times. We're going to make mistakes, and the reality is that we are all hypocrites because we can't be perfect, and we need to be honest about that. But if we pause, if we open the window of our hearts and let the Light shine on us and put our faith in the right thing – in Jesus – the whole game changes because He is the living water. With His active presence soaking deep into the roots of our spirit, we will thrive when the environment around us dries our bones. Our spirits will flourish, and hey, a flower might even begin to blossom.

When our confidence shifts from the confidence we have in ourselves to the confidence in what God can do through us, we can **boldly** live out *God's purpose* for our life instead of *people's preference* for our life. And that? That isn't just surviving – it's thriving.

So, get up little cactus, He's not done with you yet.

TALK IT OUT

Do you ever feel like the cactus in my windowsill – dry and barely surviving?

What about the college scene has encouraged or discouraged you?

If you haven't stepped into a personal relationship with God, what holds you back? Fear of rejection? Being too busy? Doubt? Discouragement? A combination?

If you have stepped into a personal relationship with God, what gives you the most anxiety or fear when it comes to living out your faith?

TRUTH SAYS...

Matthew 24:14 reminds us of the importance of following Jesus. If we are not concerned about proclaiming His good news to the kingdom throughout the world, if we're not concerned with sharing His love with others, then we are likely just surviving when we could be thriving. Faith can only flourish when we put it into action.

John 4:14 tells us that when we fill our hearts with His truth and love, it's better than the water we need to simply survive physically. If we drink from His cup, we will have *eternal, abundant* life, and we will not dry out.

Romans 12:2 is the powerful reminder to follow Christ over the crowd. When we conform to the world, we stifle our spiritual growth and shut ourselves out of the Light. We are just getting by but not really living. But when we are transformed by God's power, He refreshes our spirits and renews our hearts so that we can thrive in His love.

THE BIG IDEA:
THRIVING WITH CHRIST > SURVIVING WITH THE CROWD

Wahoo!

You made it through 42 weeks of study AND a guide for being a light on your campus!

You go girl!

My greatest prayer is that you weren't just inspired but transformed – even in the littlest of ways. I pray you connected with God, were encouraged in truth, and empowered to keep walking with Jesus.

I know, it's not easy in college; it's actually really hard. But I believe you can do hard things because of Christ who gives you strength (Philippians 4:13).

Just remember, college is temporary. Jesus is forever.
Keep fighting the good fight, Soul Sister. It's what you were made to do. You are an image bearer, a witness, and a Light warrior for His Kingdom. So, fight for it – fight like a GIRL – full of passion, purpose, and power.

Xo,
Jordan Lee

For more, follow me online!
Facebook: **Jordan Lee**
Instagram: **@soulscripts**
www.thesoulscripts.com

Acknowledgments

LEADER GUIDE
1. Tim Keller. *The Meaning of Marriage: Facing the Complexities of Commitment with the Wisdom of God.* Westminster: Penguin Books, 2013.

PARTY ON PURPOSE
1. Sheila Walsh. *The Storm Inside: Trade the Chaos of How You Feel for the Truth of Who You Are.* Scotland: Thomas Nelson, 2014.

CHILL OUT
1. Bob Goff. *Love Does: Discover a Secretly Incredible Life in an Ordinary World.* Scotland: Thomas Nelson, 2012.
2. Vince Lombardi. https://www.brainyquote.com/quotes/quotes/v/vincelomba122285.html

PERFECTER>PERFECTION
1. Jon Jorgeson. https://www.youtube.com/watch?v=uWi5iXnguTU

IT'S COMPLICATED
1. Joseph Murphy and Tim Keller. "The Miracle Power of Your Mind." https://www.youtube.com/watch? Your v=CPPvNOj9tuA

THE STRUGGLE IS REAL
1. David Platt. *Radical: Taking Back Your Faith from the American Dream.* Colorado Springs: Multnomah, 2010.
2. Tim Keller, Pastor of Redeemer Church

3. Joanna Weaver. *Having a Mary Heart in a Martha World: Finding Intimacy with God in the Busyness of Life.* Colorado Springs: WaterBrook, 2000.
4. Ibid.

SOCIAL MEDIA
1. Caroline Gregoire. "Research Links Addictive Social Media Behavior With Substance Abuse." http://www.huffingtonpost.com/2014/12/13/social-media-addiction_n_6302814.html

THIS CHANGES EVERYTHING
1. River Valley Church, Everyday Resurrection Sermon Series. http://rivervalley.net/wp-content/uploads/2016/06/160529.mp3, 11:40 mark
2. River Valley Church, Everyday Resurrection Sermon Series. http://rivervalley.net/wp-content/uploads/2016/06/160529.mp3, 15:00 mark
3. River Valley Church, Everyday Resurrection Sermon Series. http://rivervalley.net/wp-content/uploads/2016/06/160529.mp3, 17:00 mark
4. Joseph Murphy. *The Miracle Power of Your Mind: The Joseph Murphy Treasury.* Westminster: TarcherPerigree, 2016.

77028235R00142

Made in the USA
Columbia, SC
14 September 2017